TEXAS FOOTBALL

YESTERDAY & TODAY ™

BILL LITTLE

FOREWORD BY MACK BROWN

WEST
SIDE
PUBLISHING

Bill Little is in his 41st year with the University of Texas Athletic Department, currently in the position of special assistant to the head football coach for communications. A Texas native (and UT class of 1965), Little has won 15 "Best in the Nation" awards from the journalism faculty of the University of Missouri and more than 20 "Best in the District" awards from the College Sports Information Directors of America. *Texas Football: Yesterday & Today*™ is his seventh book on Texas athletics.

Mack Brown is the head football coach of the Texas Longhorns, a position he has held since 1998. He took the Longhorns to the BCS national championship in 2005 and has finished with the Longhorns ranked in the Top 10 six of his first eleven years. Twice while at Texas, he has been named "Coach of the Year" by national organizations. On October 27, 2007, Brown joined the elite company of Longhorn legend Darrell Royal, becoming the only other Texas coach to lead the football team to 100 victories.

Factual verification by Jake Veyhl.

Special thanks to UT memorabilia collectors Frank Denius and Scott Wilson for generously opening their memorabilia collections to us.

We would also like to thank Joy Lawrence at the Athletic Department of the University of Texas, and Aryn Glazier and Margaret Schlankey at the Dolph Briscoe Center for American History for their assistance with photos.

Yesterday & Today is a trademark of Publications International, Ltd.

West Side Publishing is a division of Publications International, Ltd.

ISBN-13: 978-1-4127-1508-9
ISBN-10: 1-4127-1508-3

Manufactured in China.

8 7 6 5 4 3 2 1

Library of Congress Control Number: 2008923002

Picture Credits:

Front cover: **The University of Texas at Austin, Athletic Department**

Back cover: **Getty Images**

AP Images: 38, 45, 56 (top), 72, 73 (bottom), 75, 80, 106, 120 (left), 121; *Austin American-Statesman:* 126 (bottom left); **Austin History Center, Austin Public Library:** PICA-08145c, 9; 02152c, 10; *Daily Texan:* 137 (bottom); **The Dolph Briscoe Center for American History:** Cactus Yearbook 1900, di_00021, 51; Malcolm Kutner, di_03239, 30 (bottom); Prints and Photographs Collection, di_03222, 8 (right), di_03220, 13 (left), di_04214, 14, di_02241, 15, di_01185, 41 (bottom); John Lang Sinclair, di_00022, 8 (left); UT Demonstrations, di_01807, 64 (bottom); UT Ephemera Collection, di_04202, 16 (top); UT Longhorn Band Records, di_04271, 43 (top right); UT Longhorn Football Program, di_04278, 34 (top left); John Yates, di_02388, 64 (top); **Jeff Etessam:** 111; **Getty Images:** 104, 108, 110, 112, 113 (bottom), 114, 131; *Sports Illustrated*, 73 (top), 122, 124, 125; Time Life Pictures, 22 (right center), 24 (left), 31, 53; **Murray Olderman:** 40; **PIL Collection:** 13 (right), 19 (bottom left), 22 (left center), 24 (right), 30 (top), 35 (top left), 41 (top), 42 (top right), 43 (top left), 52 (bottom), 54, 55, 60, 61, 66 (right), 70, 71, 77, 78, 79, 86, 87, 91, 93 (left), 94, 95, 97, 102, 103, 118, 119 (top right & bottom right), 120 (right), 126 (top center, top right & bottom right), 127 (top left, top right & bottom right), 128, 136, 137 (top left & top center); **University of Notre Dame Archives:** 21; **The University of Texas at Austin, Athletic Department:** 3, 7, 11, 12, 16 (bottom), 17, 18, 19 (top left, bottom center & bottom right), 20, 23, 25, 26, 27, 28, 29, 32, 33, 34 (bottom & top right), 35 (top right & bottom), 36, 37, 39, 42 (top left & bottom), 43 (left center & right center), 44, 46, 47, 48, 49, 50, 52 (top), 56 (bottom), 57, 58, 59, 62, 63, 65, 66 (left), 67, 68, 69, 74, 76, 81, 82, 83, 84, 85, 88, 89, 90, 92, 93 (right), 96, 97, 98, 99, 100, 101, 105, 107, 109, 113 (top), 115, 116, 117, 119 (bottom left), 123, 126 (top left), 127 (bottom left), 129, 130, 132, 133, 134, 135, 137 (top right)

Memorabilia photography: PDR Productions, Inc./Peter Rossi; Jim Sigmon

The Texas Longhorns take the field at Darrell K Royal–Texas Memorial Stadium in Austin with drama and authority.

Contents

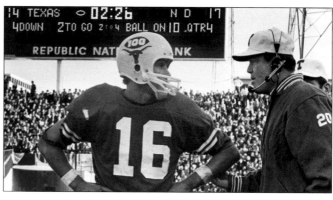

James Street and Darrell Royal p. 69

Foreword 6

The Early Years 8

The Beginning 10

Clyde Littlefield and the Early Golden Era . . . 12

Bringing Order to the Southwest 14

A Real, Live Mascot 15

The Concrete Dream 16

Koy, Stafford Lead the Longhorns
  into the '30s 17

Texas Memories 18

Jack Chevigny and the Miracle Win
  over Notre Dame 20

Bible and Beyond 22

Stepping Up to the Big Time 24

The Rivalries 26

Crain's Run 28

The Immortal 13 29

Dreams of Roses 30

The War 32

The Tower Lights 33

Texas Memories 34

The Legend of Bobby Layne . . 36

Blair Cherry 38

Ed Price 40

Memories of 1955 41

Texas Memories 42

The Royal Years 44

Beginning the Royal Era 46

Tilling the Soil: Royal's Legend Begins 48

Triumphing over Tragedy 50

Texas Orange and White 51

Going All the Way 52

Texas Memories 54

Tommy Nobis Takes on Joe Namath 56

The Mid-1960s Doldrums 57

The Wishbone 58

Texas Memories 60

Integration 62

The Loyal Lieutenants 63

Frank Erwin and the Tree Huggers 64

James Street Rises to the Occasion 65

The Game of the Century 66

The Littlest Longhorn 68

The Irish Are Coming 69

Texas Memories 70

The Texas-Oklahoma Golden Hat Trophy p. 27

A Second Year at the Top 72
A Growing Stadium for a Growing Team 74
Royalisms 75
Royal's Last Lap 76
Texas Memories 78

Grasping for the Brass Ring . 80

Akers Comes to Texas. 82
Greatness in '77 83
The Longhorns' First Heisman 84
Texas Memories 86
The Need for Speed 88
Entering the '80s. 89
Flirting with No. 1. 90
Dodds Oversees Longhorn Excellence 92
Into the Valley. 93
Texas Memories 94
The Homecoming. 96
Shock the Nation 98

John Mackovic: A New Direction 99
North vs. South. 100
Texas Memories 102

Mack Brown's in Town 104

Brown Arrives in Austin 106
Williams Runs Away with the '98 Season . . . 108
The Stadium Grows Again 110
Come Early. Be Loud.
    Stay Late. 111
Mack Brown and Darrell Royal:
    Pupil and Mentor 112
The Iconic Major Applewhite . . 114
The 1999 Recruits 116
Texas Memories 118
Cracking the BCS in 2004. 120
The 2005 Dream Season. 122
Reaching Perfection! 124
Texas Memories 126
The Amazing Vince Young 128
Supporting High School
    Coaches. 130
Turning on the Star Power. 131
Colt McCoy Takes Up the Mantle. 132
The Future at DKR. 133
The Unexpected Season of 2008. 134
Texas Memories 136

Texas Through the Years . . 138

Index 143

Adrian Walker
p. 98

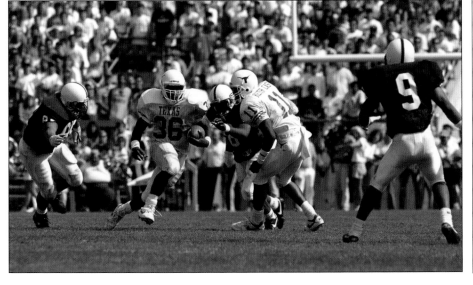

Limas Sweed
p. 122

Foreword

With a dad who owned a sporting goods store and a granddad who was the winningest high school football coach in Middle Tennessee history, it was easy for me to grow up with a love for the history of the game. My first memory of organized football is of riding a school bus, wearing my letter jacket, sitting beside my granddad on the way to a game. I think I was about six years old.

By the time I was growing up in the 1960s, television was bringing the biggest college games into our home in Cookeville, Tennessee, and I would learn about coaches in the southeastern United States such as Wally Butts at Georgia, Bobby Dodd at Georgia Tech, and Paul "Bear" Bryant at Alabama.

On the national scene, however, there was a guy down in Texas who captured the imagination of the whole country, and growing up in a coaching family, I didn't take long to make him a hero. His name was Darrell Royal. So to me, Texas football became about history and tradition a long time ago. That is why, when I first talked to my friend, Bill Little, about this book, I was happy to endorse it. There is no greater legacy in sports than that of Texas Longhorn football.

When my wife, Sally, and I came to Austin in 1998, the first thing we wanted to do was to bring back that tradition. We wanted to understand it; we wanted our players to understand it. A lot of people talked to me about the "pressure" of being the head football coach at the University of Texas. But what I came to learn was that Texas football isn't about pressure, it's about passion.

This book reflects that. It begins with some of the earliest moments of football in the Southwest, and it includes the great moments of the young guys who have played for us in the 21st century. You will meet war heroes and learn little-known facts. You will have a chance to get to know families with great bloodlines such as Ernie Koy, who played in the 1930s, and his sons, Ernie and Ted, both of whom later played professional football. Each chapter spans an era, and each, in its own way, captures a window of history.

You will come to understand the significance of the history of Darrell K Royal–Texas Memorial Stadium, which has grown from a concrete dream in the 1920s to the largest stadium in this part of the country. Most of all, however, in pictures, memorabilia, and words, *Texas Football: Yesterday & Today*™ includes a vision of the times and the people.

For the 2008 football season, our theme was, "You have to be consistently good to be great." When I look back at that idea, the choice was perfect . . . not only for that season, but for all of the things that the Texas football program stands for.

One thing I realized after coming here from North Carolina was that we all had some work to do to get that consistency back. The first thing we needed to do was to reach out to the Texas high school coaches, because they

are really the ones who lay the groundwork for any success of those of us in the college game. The second thing was to get Coach Royal and our lettermen involved again. Finally, we could not have accomplished what we have without the help and support of the university's administration, the whole athletics department, and our great fan base.

We based our program at Texas on three things: communication, trust, and respect. That went for recruits and their parents, as well as our dealings with everyone associated with the program. Any success we have enjoyed has been driven by those principles.

During the 2008 season, Texas football surpassed Notre Dame as the second winningest program (behind only Michigan) in the history of college football. Again, it was a tribute to the players and coaches who came before us and to the young men who entrusted their careers as players to us over the last 11 seasons.

Those of us who have had the privilege to coach at Texas are stewards of a legacy that existed long before we came and will be there long after we are gone. Dana X. Bible and Coach Royal brought the program to excellence in the middle part of the 20th century—with all that they accomplished, they ensured that those of us who have the honor of standing where they stood do so with responsibility. In that sense, this book is about Texas football, yesterday and today—honoring the past, celebrating the present, and looking forward to the future.

Mack Brown

Mack Brown

Mack Brown became the University of Texas football coach in 1998 and has led the Longhorns to at least nine wins in each of his 11 seasons. His 2005 team won the BCS National Championship. He has been named coach of the year by national organizations twice, in 2005 and 2008.

The Early Years

1893–1936

The rugged nature of the sport—this game called football—fit the pride of the people of Texas and the spirit of the land. The University of Texas was a small college in Austin at the turn of the 20th century. It was a time of great expectations, unforeseen challenges, and surprising rewards.

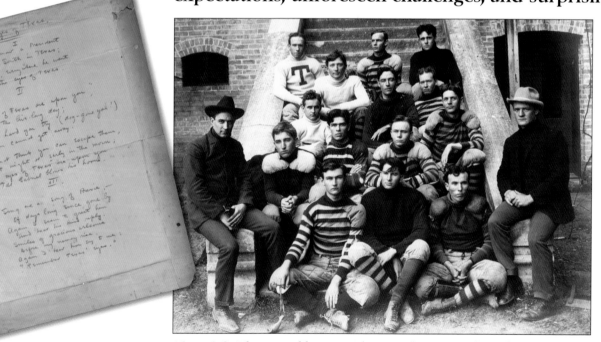

Above left: *The original lyrics to "The Eyes of Texas," performed at a student spring celebration talent show.* **Above:** *An early version of "Varsity" (what the team was called prior to adopting "Longhorns"). Uniforms were becoming the style, and the letter* T *was beginning to signal recognition for the Austin team.*

They called it football, but it looked more like an organized scrum as Texas pushed for a score in the early years. Notice the referee, in a shirt and tie, and the wooden goal posts.

The Beginning

When the train pulled out of Austin the night before Thanksgiving Day, 1893, it had 15 or so "wannabe" football players and a couple of hundred fans from the University of Texas onboard for a ride toward destiny. At the end of the line in Dallas, the most feared team in the area waited for a showdown.

The Dallas Foot Ball Club, the self-proclaimed "Champions of Texas," had heard that an upstart group from the college down in Austin was trying to put together a football team. So they issued a challenge: "Come on up."

Football had evolved since that first 1869 college game between Princeton and Rutgers. Then, 50 or so players

The very first Texas football team is seen in an 1893 photograph. Front row (l-r): *Dave Furman, Bill McLean, Walt Crawford (manager), Dick Lee, Addison Day.* Middle row: *Victor Moore, Paul McLane, John Philp.* Back row: *Ray McLane, Jim Morrison, "Baby" Myers, Robert Roy.*

pulled off their coats and engaged in what amounted to a primitive game of soccer. By 1893, the number of colleges with football teams had grown to 88, and the game had been scaled down: Each team allowed 11 players at any one time on the playing field, which was 110 yards long.

The ride to Dallas took most of the night, and when the engine chugged into the station at daybreak, the brash youngsters got off and headed for Fairgrounds Park. They let the vaunted Dallasites know they meant business, too.

"When we got there," recalled guard Billy Richardson, "we all bought big cigars and strutted down Main Street."

The University of Texas was considerably different then than it is now. There were only a couple of buildings on campus, and Austin itself had just 15,000 residents. The $30 university tuition allowed a student to attend as long as was needed in a particular course of study.

But while the Dallas Foot Ball Club had its reputation, the young men from down in Austin had youth, enthusiasm, and a team full of colorful characters, including a cowboy from Ballinger, Texas, named Addison "Ad" Day. Not only was he the team's main rusher, he was the first kicker in school history. In those days, a field goal was worth five points, while a touchdown produced only four. A successful goal-after-touchdown (free kick) earned two.

The Dallas Morning News assessed the game this way: "To a man who has never heard of Walter Camp and doesn't know a halfback from a tackle, the professional game of foot ball looks very much like an Indian wrestling match with a lot of running thrown in."

Ad Day was the hero, kicking three extra points and scoring two touchdowns as the college boys stunned the crusty veterans of the vaunted Dallas Foot Ball Club, 18–16. University of Texas football had its first victory.

Over the next dozen years, the sport, the university, and its team evolved. As the young university came of age, milestones included a victory in its first college game (38–0 over rival Texas A&M in 1894) and the creation of a mascot that became a worldwide symbol of the school.

Known only as "Varsity" in its early years, the team got a new moniker from a student writer named D. A. Frank in *The Daily Texan*, the school paper. In 1903, Frank began calling the team "the Texas Longhorns," reasoning that through constant usage, the name would stick. By 1906 it was in constant use, but the name didn't become firmly established until 1913, when H. J. Lutcher Stark, a former student and team manager, gave the squad a number of orange-and-white blankets emblazoned with the *Texas Longhorns* moniker.

The year 1903 also saw the creation of another great Texas tradition. University president William Lambdin Prather, more commonly known as Colonel Prather, had attended Virginia's Washington College (known today as Washington and Lee University) and was a great admirer of its president, Robert E. Lee. Prather recalled that Lee often told his students, "The eyes of the South are upon you," which he borrowed and paraphrased in his own speeches as, "The eyes of Texas are upon you." That saying gained greater life courtesy of John Sinclair, a student who took the music to "I've Been Working on the Railroad" for a spoof in a college show that began, "The eyes of Texas are upon you." Although intended as a parody, the song was taken seriously and became the Texas alma mater.

With that, all of the pieces were in place. The eyes of Texas, and the eyes of the growing college football community, would soon be on the University of Texas Longhorns.

Henry Reeves

Dressed in a black suit and a black Stetson hat, Henry Reeves influenced the Longhorns football team as much as anyone in the first 20 years of Texas athletics.

Reeves was born the son of freed slaves. No one really knew when he came to Texas, but he seemed to be a fixture from the beginning. He carried a medicine bag, a towel, and a water bucket. He ultimately became almost as well known as the football team itself. The cries of "Time out for Texas," and "Water, Henry," brought the familiar sight of his tall, dark figure moving quickly onto the field. There he would kneel beside a fallen player and patch a cut or soothe a sore muscle.

From 1895 to 1915, "Doc" Henry was the trainer, the masseuse, and the closest thing to a doctor the fledgling football team ever knew. In a time when an African American could not attend the University of Texas or, for that matter, eat at the same table with the players he treated, Reeves was called "the most famous character connected with football in the University of Texas."

As the team boarded a train to College Station to play the Aggies in 1915, however, Doc Henry felt a numbness that all his self-taught medical  knowledge couldn't cure. By halftime, the stroke that would ultimately kill him had paralyzed the lanky trainer. When he died, the entire student body took up a collection to pay his medical expenses, and *The Houston Post* published a tribute to him. He was inducted posthumously into the Longhorn Hall of Honor in 2000.

Clyde Littlefield and the Early Golden Era

One of the most important figures in Texas athletics was Clyde Littlefield, shown here during his football playing days in the mid-1910s. Littlefield was an All-America basketball player and a track star as well. He went on to become the Longhorns' head football coach, as well as one of the greatest track-and-field coaches in NCAA history.

As Texas football came of age in the pre–World War I era, the university created heroes who became part of the fiber of the school. Perhaps the most significant of these was a lanky youngster named Clyde Littlefield.

When Littlefield and his future teammates arrived at Texas in the second decade of the 20th century, college football was coming out of a serious crisis. In 1905, the rough style of play, coupled with the lack of helmets and adequate protection for the body, had produced so many deaths and injuries that schools such as Columbia, Northwestern, California, and Stanford either dropped the sport altogether or played rugby instead.

So serious was the situation that President Theodore Roosevelt called representatives from the Big Three—Harvard, Princeton, and Yale—to the White House and basically ordered them to tone down the savage nature of the game. The result of that meeting was a number of rule changes, including one that revolutionized play—the addition of the forward pass. For a young Clyde Littlefield, that meant a ticket to a whole new ball game.

In the first 18 years of football at the University of Texas, 13 different men had served as the team's head coach. It appeared that Billy Wasmund, a former University of Michigan quarterback, was going to bring some stability when he took over the program in 1910, but just before the 1911 season was to begin, he fell off a balcony while apparently sleepwalking and died. Assistants such as William J. "Billy" Disch, who became a legend as the Texas baseball coach, took over until UT hired Dave Allerdice, Wasmund's former Michigan teammate, as head football coach.

Allerdice's success—he was 33–7 from 1911 through 1915—made up the golden era of early Texas football. And his brightest star was Clyde Littlefield, who became extremely adept at throwing the forward pass.

At 6'1" and 180 pounds, Littlefield became the university's first superstar. He earned 12 letters in football, basketball, and track from 1912 through 1916, and he would have lettered in baseball if he'd just had a little more time to devote to it. In a streak that began in the middle of the 1912 season and extended through the third game of 1915, Allerdice and Littlefield teamed up to carry Texas to a remarkable 23–1 record. The only blemish came in a 30–7 loss to Notre Dame in the final game of 1913, a game that featured future Fighting Irish coach Knute Rockne as a player.

During Littlefield's time, the Texas basketball team also went on a 44-game winning streak, which still ranks among the longest in NCAA history. Littlefield was named a Helms Foundation All-American in basketball and was the leading scorer in both basketball and football during the inaugural year of the Southwest Conference. In track, he lost only one collegiate race and equaled the world record for 120-yard high hurdles.

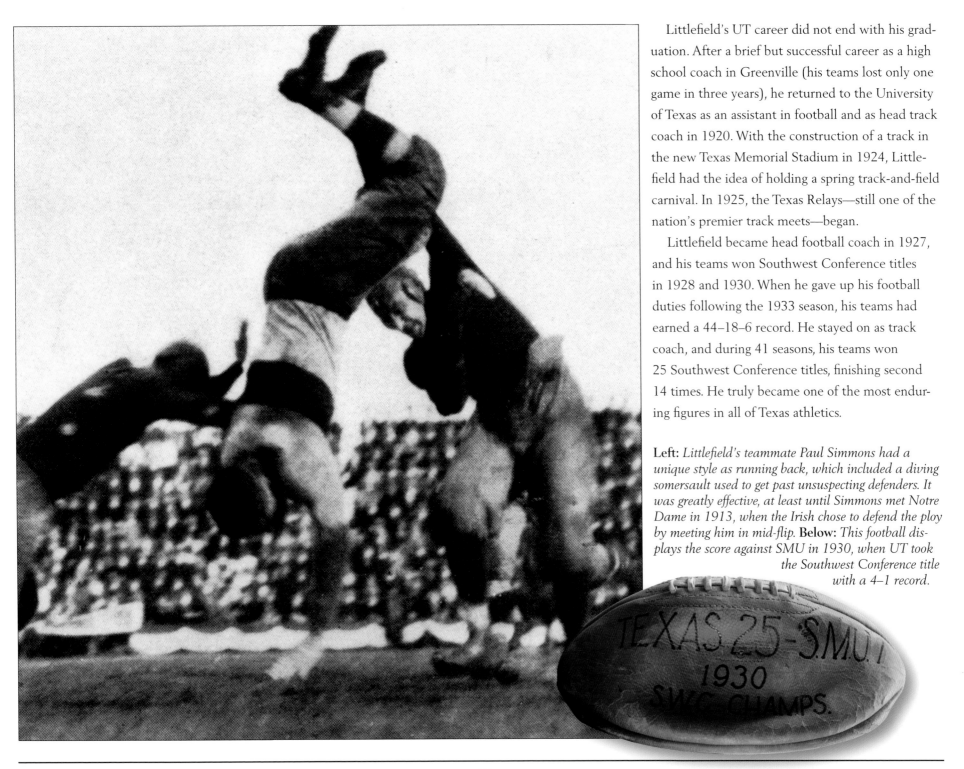

Littlefield's UT career did not end with his graduation. After a brief but successful career as a high school coach in Greenville (his teams lost only one game in three years), he returned to the University of Texas as an assistant in football and as head track coach in 1920. With the construction of a track in the new Texas Memorial Stadium in 1924, Littlefield had the idea of holding a spring track-and-field carnival. In 1925, the Texas Relays—still one of the nation's premier track meets—began.

Littlefield became head football coach in 1927, and his teams won Southwest Conference titles in 1928 and 1930. When he gave up his football duties following the 1933 season, his teams had earned a 44–18–6 record. He stayed on as track coach, and during 41 seasons, his teams won 25 Southwest Conference titles, finishing second 14 times. He truly became one of the most enduring figures in all of Texas athletics.

Left: *Littlefield's teammate Paul Simmons had a unique style as running back, which included a diving somersault used to get past unsuspecting defenders. It was greatly effective, at least until Simmons met Notre Dame in 1913, when the Irish chose to defend the ploy by meeting him in mid-flip.* **Below:** *This football displays the score against SMU in 1930, when UT took the Southwest Conference title with a 4–1 record.*

Bringing Order to the Southwest

Taming the land had been a large part of the pioneer days of Texas. Although that was largely behind Texans by the early 1900s, the frontier seemed to live on in the disorder of college athletics in the second decade of the 20th century.

L. Theo Bellmont was the university's first athletics director and a driving force in the creation of the Southwest Conference. The building under the west side of Darrell K Royal–Texas Memorial Stadium is named for Bellmont.

The University of Texas first became involved with a league just two years into its football competition, when in 1895 it joined the Southern Intercollegiate Athletic Association (SIAA), which spanned the entire South and included a multitude of colleges and universities. By 1904, the disenchanted folks in Austin withdrew from what had become an early version of a "mega-conference." But Texas actually had dual conference memberships, participating not only in the SIAA but in the Texas Intercollegiate Athletic Association (TIAA), as well. Also in the mix was the Southwestern Intercollegiate Athletic Association (SWIAA), a league that included Texas, Texas A&M, and other Texas schools as well as Oklahoma, Missouri School of Mines, and Washington University of St. Louis.

Soon, however, the SWIAA had withered, and the only remaining effort at a stable league was the TIAA, which was centered mostly around an annual spring track meet. Unfortunately the membership kept changing. More significantly, the league's admission standards and eligibility rules were too lax for the larger institutions.

By 1913, University of Texas athletics director L. Theo Bellmont had become frustrated with practices that saw first-year students, transfers, and graduate students immediately eligible to compete. Such policies left room for irregularities—the most significant of which allowed players to enroll in school only for the football season. So Bellmont and Dr. W. T. Mather, chairman of the UT Athletics Council, took action, sending out letters to all of the larger institutions in the southwestern United States to gauge interest in forming a new league that would set appropriate standards.

A number of them responded with interest. On May 6, 1914, representatives of eight schools met at the Oriental Hotel in Dallas to form the Southwest Intercollegiate Athletic Conference, which later became the Southwest Conference. The new league limited athletes to three varsity seasons after a year of residence and installed a strict amateur code. On December 8, 1914, the SWC was formally organized at the Rice Hotel in Houston, with charter members the University of Texas, Texas A&M, Baylor University, Southwestern University, the University of Arkansas, the University of Oklahoma, and Oklahoma A&M. Rice was accepted but backed out of the league for 1916 and 1917. Representatives from LSU came to the meeting and listened but didn't join.

The league ultimately took a form that included Texas, Texas A&M, Baylor, Arkansas, Texas Christian University, Southern Methodist University, and Rice. Texas Technological College (which later changed its name to Texas Tech University) joined in the late 1950s, and the University of Houston became a member during the 1970s.

A Real, Live Mascot

Members of the the UT alumni organization, Texas Exes, had long wanted to present the university with an actual Texas longhorn steer as the college mascot. One alum, Stephen Pinckney, had gone to work for the U.S. attorney general chasing down cattle rustlers. After one raid, he came across a steer colored the perfect shade of orange. Using money collected from other alumni, he bought it and had it shipped to Austin.

The new mascot debuted at halftime of the 1916 game against Texas A&M on Thanksgiving Day. Perhaps inspired by the living, breathing longhorn in their midst, the Longhorn football team took the day by a score of 21–7. Touting the gift in the December issue of the alumni magazine, *The Alcalde*, editor Ben Dyer wrote, "His name is Bevo. Long may he reign." No one knows precisely where Dyer came up with the name Bevo.

In fact, the origin of the name has been the subject of some controversy over the years. One widely believed story suggests it originated in a brand given to the steer by a stray group of Aggies early in 1917. Possibly still smarting from their Thanksgiving Day loss, the vandals seared the score of the previous season's game, a 13–0 win by the Aggies, into the longhorn's side. Attempting to cover the insult, so the story goes, Texas students altered the 13 to a *B*, the dash to an *E*, and added a *V* in front of the *0*. Although Texas A&M enjoys taking credit for the name, no one altered the brand. In fact, the first Bevo was fattened for a football banquet. Attendees from Texas A&M were served from the side that carried the mark and were given the branded hide to take home with them.

There have been several steers over the years to take the name of Bevo. The most recent, Bevo XIV, was introduced during the first game of the 2004 season. Did the presence of a brand-new longhorn mascot inspire its football-playing namesakes? No one can know for sure, but Texas defeated the University of North Texas 65–0.

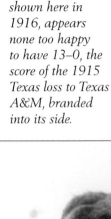

The original Bevo, shown here in 1916, appears none too happy to have 13–0, the score of the 1915 Texas loss to Texas A&M, branded into its side.

The Concrete Dream

Below: The 1924 Thanksgiving match between Texas and Texas A&M served as the stadium's Dedication Game. The doughboy depicted on the day's program is a reminder that the structure was intended to honor Texan veterans of World War I.
Bottom: *Texas Memorial Stadium as it looked on its Dedication Day. Two years later, a concrete north end was built, adding 14,000 seats.*

The idea of a concrete stadium to replace the wooden bleachers at old Clark Field had actually been stirred in 1923, when Athletics Director Theo Bellmont had held a meeting with 30 student leaders at the university cafeteria. That prompted a general meeting of the entire student body, and from there the idea went to the Board of Regents.

The cause was twofold. First, it was to build a facility the likes of which had not been seen in the Southwest. And second, it was to honor the 198,293 Texans who had served in World War I, being dedicated to the 5,280 who died. The name Texas Memorial Stadium recognized all Texans in the war, not just those who went to the University of Texas. Students led the fundraising effort toward a subscription goal of $500,000.

Dynamite blasted away the rock of a 13-acre tract on a hillside east of Waller Creek between 20th and 23rd streets; horse-drawn equipment hauled the dirt away. Excavation for the construction began the first of April, 1924, with the objective of having a 27,000-seat stadium finished by Thanksgiving. On November 8, before a crowd of 13,500, Texas played Baylor in the site's very first game.

Just as the builders had planned, the stadium was dedicated a few weeks later, when a record 33,000, including folks in bleachers at the north and south end, watched Texas beat Texas A&M, 7–0.

The original construction consisted of just the east and west stands. Though it has been remodeled several times since, that core remains today.

Heroes of the War

World War I, in which the United States fought in 1917 and 1918, had quite an impact on Texas. Among the more than 5,000 Texans who lost their lives were four Longhorn football players. When Texas Memorial Stadium was dedicated in 1924, the names of those four were immortalized on a plaque at the entrance to the field.

The first to die was Louis Jordan, popular captain of the 1914 Longhorns, from wounds suffered when an artillery shell hit his position in the Luneville sector of France on March 5, 1918. Bothwell Kane, a lineman on the 1912 team, was also killed by an artillery shell on July 28 at the Ourcq River crossing at Villers Surs Fere. James Higginbotham, another member of the 1912 team, died in an airplane training accident before departing for France. The final Longhorn death in World War I was that of James "Pete" Edmond, one of the school's best athletes from 1913 through 1916 and the recipient of a Silver Star for gallantry in September 1918. He was killed by machine-gun fire in the battle of the Argonne Forest on October 11, 1918—just a month before the war ended.

Koy, Stafford Lead the Longhorns into the '30s

Ernie Koy—the patriarch of a family that would also see sons Ernie and Ted star at Texas—was outstanding both in football and baseball in the early 1930s.

In the last few years of the 1920s, Coach Clyde Littlefield led Texas to respectable, if not stellar, seasons. But after a completely mediocre Southwest Conference record of 2–2–2 in 1929 and the prospects of a totally different team the next year with running back Dexter Shelley as the only returning starter, the future looked bleak.

As the 1930 season began, however, Longhorn football suddenly did not look so dire. Unexpected football players emerged to lead Texas into an age of legends. Ernie Koy had come to UT from Sealy, Texas, to play baseball, but it didn't take long for Koy to prove himself a star on the football field, as well. And assistant coach C. J. "Shorty" Alderson had a discovery of his own. On the first day of practice, he raced from the freshman practice field to find Littlefield at the stadium.

"Clyde," he said, "I've found the darndest football player you ever saw. He tore up a couple of dummies and hurt a couple of men. He says his name is Harrison Stafford."

Koy, Stafford, and Shelley were joined by Ox Emerson, Wilson "Bull" Elkins, Ox Blanton, and Lester Peterson—most of whom would make All-Southwest Conference—on a team that won the league and recorded an 8–1–1 season. With Stafford blocking, Koy running on offense, and a defense that pitched a remarkable seven shutouts, the 1930 team ranked among the best in the university's first half-century of competition.

Stafford's rugged play became known throughout the Southwest. Against TCU in 1932, his block on future Ole Miss Coach Johnny Vaught earned incredible reviews. "The sound of the collision," wrote the *Fort Worth Star-Telegram*, "could be heard all over the field. . . [Vaught] went down as though shot, his headgear jumping half off his head."

Stafford and Koy established themselves as Texas legends: Stafford went on to be inducted into the National Football Foundation's College Hall of Fame, and Koy would prosper with a professional baseball career following his time at Texas.

Littlefield's success continued through the 1932 season. By 1933, however, Stafford, Koy, and 14 other lettermen were gone, and the Longhorns struggled to a 4–5–2 season. With that, Littlefield chose to resign his football coaching position. He stayed on with the university as track coach.

As a runner, blocker, and tackler, Harrison Stafford was one of the toughest players in Texas history.

This handbill announced the first-ever football game featuring the University of Texas. This game may also have started what has often been a fine Longhorn tradition: a Thanksgiving Day football game.

It wasn't just Oklahoma who played UT at the Texas State Fair. This game against Vanderbilt took place in a wooden stadium that predated the Cotton Bowl.

The Sewanee Tigers, also called the Iron Men, came to Austin as the first stop on a whirlwind tour. They defeated the Longhorns 12–0, the first of five shutouts Sewanee won in six days, on their way to a final undefeated record of 12–0 in 1899.

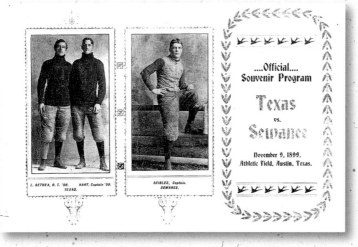

Thanksgiving Day often meant a game against Texas A&M. This year, the home crowd in Austin saw a 14–5 Longhorn victory.

A Chicago newspaper cartoonist captured the pregame mood of the 1904 Texas game against the University of Chicago, helping fire up coach Amos Alonzo Stagg's team. It worked. Chicago beat the out-gunned Texans 68–0.

Steers Tame Fighting Irish 7–6
Saturday, October 6, 1934
Notre Dame Held to Two Field Goals

The contest, held at Notre Dame Stadium in South Bend, Indiana, was over almost before it began when Irish receivers fumbled the starting kickoff. Longhorn Jack Gray recovered the ball inside the Irish 20, and four plays later, running back Bohn Hilliard triumphantly carried it across the goal line for the only touchdown the Longhorns needed. The extra point brought Texas to 7 points, and from there, the defense did the rest. Notre Dame never entered their own end zone, and two field goals were the only scores the South Bend team could put on the board.

OFFICIAL PROGRAM

TEXAS vs OKLAHOMA

October 10, 1936   Price 25c

The Red River rivalry between the University of Texas and Oklahoma University could (and still can) always promise to heat up state loyalties.

STATE FAIR STADIUM

FOOTBALL

TEXAS UNIV. VS. OKLAHOMA UNIV.

Saturday, Oct. 14, 1933   3:00 P. M.

PRICE $2.00

Sec. **7**   Row **11**   Seat **8**

ADMIT ONE—No Cash Refund will be made on this ticket.

It is not known whether this ticket was held by a supporter of UT or OU, but the bearer saw the Sooners shut out the Longhorns 9–0.

A game ball commemorates another Thanksgiving Day win by Texas, this time in an away game at A&M.

Jack Chevigny and the Miracle Win over Notre Dame

Handsome Jack Chevigny cut a dashing figure when he became the Texas head coach in 1934.

Clyde Littlefield had been a major part of Texas football for more than 20 years when he elected to step aside as head football coach, and his choice left the university with a decision to make. Littlefield had brought a degree of stability to the program and was respected and genuinely liked. But Texas fans had begun grousing that he was "too nice" to get the job done in the toughening world of college football.

Jack Chevigny was one of the great names in Notre Dame history. He had been a protégé of the late Knute Rockne. In the famous "Win One for the Gipper" game against Army in 1928, Chevigny scored an important touchdown and is said to have exclaimed, "There's one for the Gipper." At one point, many thought that Chevigny might follow Rockne as coach for the Fighting Irish.

Instead, here he was, coaching at St. Edward's University, a little college just south of the Colorado River in Austin whose priests came from the same Catholic order as Notre Dame. It had previously been the proving ground for Longhorn baseball when Texas had looked south to find wildly successful head coach Billy Disch. Now another opportunity seemed to come knocking. The University of Texas convinced Chevigny, with great looks and sleek black hair, to move a few miles north to its campus for the 1934 season.

"Handsome Jack" brought a lot of flashy style and showmanship to the coaching job. When he was hired, he proclaimed, "I shall do my best to make the flag of Texas fly high among those of the schools in the nation."

Among the innovations he brought that season was the first network broadcast of a Southwest Conference game when Texas played Rice in Houston. He also inaugurated the Orange-White spring intrasquad game as part of the festive "Round Up" activities on campus, drawing 4,000 fans to the contest.

But Chevigny's greatest moment might have come early in his Texas career. By chance, the Longhorns were scheduled to play Notre Dame in their second game of 1934. Chevigny's team had opened with a 12–6 victory over Texas Tech, and as the Longhorns prepared to head to South Bend, a pep rally drew more than 6,000 students. Spirit and hopes were high, but pragmatists thought defeats similar to the 30–7 and 36–7 losses Texas had previously suffered at the hands of the Irish in Austin two decades earlier might be more likely.

Chevigny delivered a masterful pregame speech, recalling his time with Rockne and speaking of his own father, who—he said—was gravely ill. He had the team so emotional that one player actually tripped because of tears in his eyes when the team burst out of the locker room.

Commemorating Chevigny's first year as coach, this review recorded an initial record of 7–2–1 overall and 4–1–1 in conference play, which was good for second place.

Running back Bohn Hilliard follows the block of guard Joe Smartt for eight yards and the only Longhorn touchdown of the game as the 1934 team stunned Notre Dame.

Notre Dame fumbled the opening kickoff, and Texas recovered at the Irish 18. Star Longhorn running back Bohn Hilliard scored the game's first touchdown on an eight-yard run. Hilliard kicked the extra point, and Texas was on its way to a stunning 7–6 victory.

Chevigny had pulled off the impossible. His team had handed Notre Dame its first-ever home-opener loss. And after the win, the young Longhorn coach was seen visiting with his father, who somehow miraculously recovered from his "illness" in time to attend the game.

The victory earned Texas a new level of respect in college football and in its own hometown. When the train carrying the team pulled into Austin at 7 A.M. the next Tuesday, a huge crowd, including soon-to-be-governor James V. Allred, was there to greet them.

The Longhorns went on to carve a 7–2–1 record that season, but Chevigny's bright light dimmed too soon. Over the next two years, the Longhorns posted back-to-back losing seasons of 4–6 and 2–6–1. By the end of 1936, the Texas coaching tenure of showman Jack Chevigny had ended.

In a time when the country was mired in the Great Depression, Chevigny gave the university and the state of Texas something to be proud of, a football milestone that has never been forgotten.

The Odd Journey of Jack Chevigny's Pen

The Longhorn players were so impressed with their victory over the Fighting Irish that they gave their coach a gold pen and pencil set engraved "To Jack Chevigny, an old Notre Damer who beat Notre Dame."

Chevigny left football when his Texas coaching career ended at the close of the 1936 season. When World War II broke out, he became a Marine officer and was killed at Iwo Jima in 1945.

When Japan surrendered a few months later, officers of the United States and Japan gathered on the battleship *Missouri* to sign the papers to end the war. One of the U.S. officers noticed a Japanese officer signing with a shiny gold fountain pen that appeared to have some English writing on it. The officer asked to see the pen, and he read the inscription: "To Jack Chevigny…"

As the story goes, the officer took the pen home to America. There he found Chevigny's sister living in Chicago and returned the pen to her.

Bible and Beyond

1937–1956

The year was 1937. The country was in the midst of the Great Depression, and so was Texas football. The dreams of national prominence that had accompanied Jack Chevigny's big win over Notre Dame three years earlier had faded. Now, it was time for a bold move. And if you want big and bold, look no further than Texas. Longhorn football was about to enter one of its finest eras.

Coaching gear was different in the 1940s. Dana X. Bible always wore coat and tie and a hat. He traditionally sat in a chair or on a bench.

"The Immortal 13" would be how folks would remember the 1940 Texas Longhorn team and their stunning 7–0 victory over No. 1 Texas A&M. Above, Pete Layden, one of the great athletes of his era, scores the only touchdown of the game.

Stepping Up to the Big Time

D. X. Bible was one of the winningest coaches in the first 50 years of the 20th century in stints at Texas A&M, Nebraska, and Texas.

The world of college football was already familiar with Dana Xenophon Bible. He had coached at Texas A&M for 11 years, posting a 72–19–9 record and winning five Southwest Conference championships. In the football season of 1936, he was firmly entrenched as the head coach at the University of Nebraska. In eight seasons there, his teams had won six Big Six championships and compiled a 50–15–7 record.

At UT, the program had gone in the wrong direction. Jack Chevigny's star as head coach had quickly tarnished after a bright beginning, and by the end of his third season, Chevigny was on his way out. The flash that had been an opening win and a very successful season in 1934 had faded. As Chevigny's third year ground to a merciful close, the Longhorns and their fans were left to ponder a

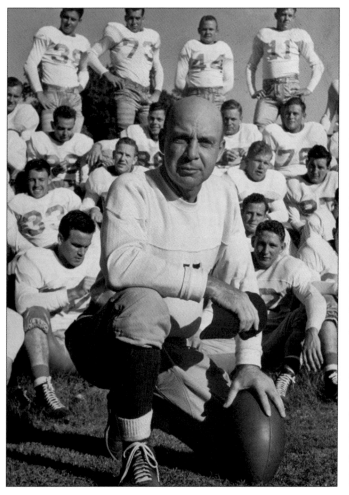

1–5 tie for the cellar in the Southwest Conference and a 2–6–1 year overall.

With three games remaining in the season, the former Notre Dame star announced that he had asked UT authorities not to reappoint him as coach when his contract ran out at the close of the season. Four days after the season ended, they took him up on that request. Now, the question they asked was, "Where do we go from here?"

Dana X. Bible was making $12,000 a year as head coach at Nebraska, $7,000 more than Texas had paid Chevigny for each of his last two seasons. But functioning without an athletics director since 1929, the Texas athletics program had become a ship sailing without a rudder.

Texans tend to think large, and influential backers had long been convinced that Bible was just the man to give the athletics program direction and make the Longhorns a winner in football. They'd had their eyes on him for some time. When Bible left Texas A&M after the 1928 season, the UT Athletics Council drafted a resolution of regret, commending him as "an exemplary sportsman both in victory and defeat."

At a secret meeting at the home of Athletics Council chairman Dr. J. C. Dolley in early December, Bible was ambushed by the Texas loyalists. Dolley had convinced the coach to come to Texas with his wife and family, and Bible considered the trip a brief vacation to visit relatives. Remembering the kindness shown him by UT upon his departure from A&M, Bible planned to suggest candidates

Taking on Heisman Trophy winner John David Crow and the Texas A&M Aggies resulted in a 34–21 loss for the '56 Longhorns, who ended the season with a 1–9 record.

The 26–12 triumph over Rice in 1939 helped Texas to its first winning season (5–4) under Bible. It was the Longhorns' first victory over the Owls in six years.

for its coaching position. Instead, Bible met with some of the most powerful people in the state who, in a session that lasted for hours, tried to convince him to take the position himself.

During Christmas holidays and the NCAA meetings that followed, Dolley continued conversations with Bible. Keeping their options open, the Athletics Council also invited Ray Morrison of Vanderbilt and Howard Jones of Southern Cal to visit. When both turned down invitations, the council put a full-court press on Bible: They recommended that he be offered a ten-year contract to accept a new role of athletics director and head football coach. He would be paid $7,500 as coach and $7,500 as athletics director for a combined salary of $15,000, almost double that of the university president and triple that of the highest-paid professor.

In January 1937, Bible accepted the offer, and the face of Texas athletics changed forever. Bible's commitment to winning on the field was well-known. What the 45-year-

old graduate of Carson-Newman College and native of Tennessee also brought, however, was something he called "The Bible Plan," which put an end to the haphazard pattern of recruiting, upgraded the school's athletics, and made a commitment of scholarship support to the student athletes until graduation.

Bible stood only 5'8" tall, but he walked as a giant in a career that covered much of the first half of the 20th century. He missed one season due to service in World War I, and his final years at Texas were affected by World War II. Still, when he retired after the 1946 season, he was the third-winningest coach in the history of the game—behind only Pop Warner and Amos Alonzo Stagg.

His players were some of the best and most colorful in Longhorn history, and his tenure was one of success and respect. To a man, his players years later would not call him by his first name or by "Coach." To them, he would forever be known simply and reverently as "Mr. Bible."

The Rivalries

Gilly Davis makes a cut in the Longhorns' victory over Texas A&M in 1938. The 7–6 triumph was the only win of the season for the 1–8 team in D. X. Bible's second year. The win preserved a home win streak in Texas Memorial Stadium against the Aggies, which would stretch from 1924 until 1956.

Over the years, the Texas Longhorns have developed two primary rivalries. One began with its roots in the land—the battle for bragging rights between two state institutions of higher education. The other became one of the most high-profile showcases in college football history. Texas played its first football game against Texas A&M in 1894, and it first met Oklahoma in 1900.

In the beginning, the Longhorns' fiercest competition came from their state neighbors only about 100 miles away in College Station. The culture of that in-state struggle dates all the way back to the days when Texas was a sovereign nation, a republic for a few years in the 1830s and '40s. It was then that the first plans were made to create what would later—in the Texas Constitution of 1876—be called "a university of the first class." Thirty years after Texas was annexed into the United States, the state legislature established a land grant college called Texas Agricultural and Mechanical College and, a few years after that, a liberal arts school known as the University of Texas was established in Austin. In 1894—just 11 years after UT first opened its doors and a year into its football program—the two schools met on the gridiron for the first time. Texas won 38–0.

The competition with Texas A&M came to a temporary halt after 1911, when angry mobs from both sides threatened the peace of Houston—where the two had met—after a 6–0 Texas victory. The UT Athletics Council canceled the series as a result, and it didn't resume until both teams played in the first year of the Southwest Athletics Conference in 1915. The games are often played on Thanksgiving Day, which has become an on-again, off-again tradition.

After A&M won its only national championship in 1939, the series took a turn decidedly in UT's favor. For the next 35 years, Texas won 31 games, A&M only 3, with one game ending in a tie. Still, the dynamic of the rivalry held, often with an unusual family-affair twist.

Until the late '60s, A&M was an all-male school with a strong military connection. An Aggie male would often marry a girl who had graduated from UT, so the "in-breeding" between rival schools made the perfect backdrop for some family feuds. When game day was on Thanksgiving, however, it also meant that folks

Thanksgiving 1940 saw another matchup against the Aggies. It was a low-scoring affair, 7–0, but it was the first contest of an eight-game Longhorn winning streak over A&M.

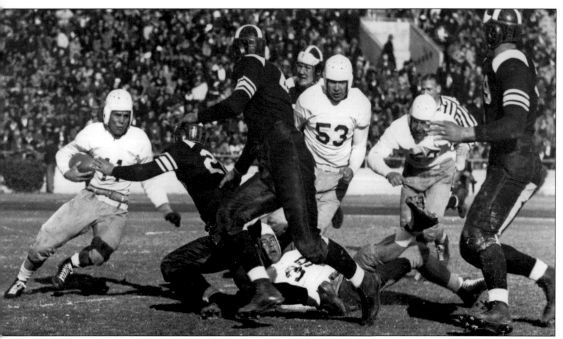

would sit down to turkey dinner and hug each other after the contest. As of the 2008 season, Texas leads the series 74–36–5.

In 1900, Oklahoma was seven years away from statehood, but its premier collegiate institution fielded a football team that traveled to Austin for the inaugural meeting between Texas and Oklahoma. It was ironic that Texas used the game, a 28–2 victory, as a warm-up for a meeting at Dallas's State Fair Park with Vanderbilt. More than a quarter of a century later, Texas ended its sporadic rivalry with Vandy in Dallas and traded that game for a State Fair date with Oklahoma—thus beginning the high-profile series we know today.

The Oklahoma series was different than the Texas A&M one. After OU's brief appearance as a member in the early years of the Southwest Conference, the Sooners went away to their own league. So for most of 90 years, Texas and Oklahoma formed the fiercest interstate rivalry in the country that wasn't played in a conference environment.

Beginning in 1929, Texas and Oklahoma met annually in Dallas, moving to the Cotton Bowl stadium when it was completed in 1937. The game soon became a staple of the State Fair of Texas, always played on the first or second weekend of October.

Unlike the Texas A&M series, where the setting was more of a "brother versus brother" civil war, the Texas-Oklahoma weekend became known as much for the party as for the game. Dallas, almost 200 miles from each campus, proved the perfect setting, and

The Texas-Oklahoma Golden Hat Trophy is presented annually by the State Fair of Texas. It travels back and forth across the Red River, depending on which team has most recently won their annual shoot-out.

"Texas-OU weekend" became part of college life at the two schools. Often, both schools would be ranked among the nation's top teams. In such years, they would meet at midseason like two warring nations and then return to their homes to try to win their conferences and secure prime bowl bids at season's end. All of that changed, however, with the formation of the Big 12 Conference in 1996, when the two schools were reunited as league siblings. Texas also leads this series as of 2008, 58–40–5.

Through the years, other members of the Southwest Conference filled the role of "rival" for a while, but none sustained the competition like Texas A&M and Oklahoma. Texas holds a 56–21 edge over Arkansas in a series that also dates back to 1894. It heated during the Darrell Royal era when his friend Frank Broyles was the Razorback coach.

The Longhorns are in hot pursuit of an Oklahoma running back during the 1946 Texas-OU game in the Cotton Bowl stadium in Dallas. Texas went on to win the game 20–13.

Crain's Run

In the beginning, winning was not easy for D. X. Bible's Longhorns. Left with the remnants of Jack Chevigny's failing final season, Bible's first team went 2–6–1. They were even worse in 1938 at 1–8–0. Cynics who decried the lack of success made a play on the title of the old Arabian Nights tale, terming the defense "Ali Bible and the Forty Sieves" because it always seemed to be leaking.

All that began to change, however, in the fourth game of 1939. Texas had opened the season with victories over Florida and Wisconsin, and the Longhorns were 2–1 as they hosted rival Arkansas, which had beaten them 42–6 a season earlier. The Razorbacks were leading 13–7 and had held Texas to just 78 yards through the first 59 minutes of the game.

Many of the 17,000 in attendance had left or were headed out of Memorial Stadium when suddenly, with only 30 seconds left, fullback R. B. Patrick faded back and flipped a short pass to Jack Crain, one of a stable of

It's another touchdown for "Cowboy Jack" Crain during the banner season of 1941. Crain, Pete Layden, and Noble Doss would become legends during the year that, for the first time ever, saw the Longhorns ranked No. 1 in the country.

1938 Frosh

It's hard to imagine in our modern world of limited scholarships, but when D. X. Bible came to Texas promising to give young men a chance to gain a college education on an athletics scholarship, he was talking about a lot of young men.

Bible's arrival early in 1937 didn't leave much time for recruiting that fall's freshman class, but he made up for it in 1938. "There were 125 of us who were part of that 1938 freshman class," recalled Noble Doss, one of the many stars in the group. "We had all-staters from all over Texas." In addition to Doss, this group included such all-time Longhorn greats as Jack Crain, Pete Layden, Malcolm Kutner, and others.

A scholarship at the time meant $40 a month, out of which the players had to pay the university $30 for room and board. The school also held out $7.50 a month to pay tuition, which left the players $2.50 a month in spending money.

1938
THE TEXAS GRIDIRON
TEXAS VS BAYLOR
PRICE 25¢

remarkable sophomores. "Cowboy Jack," as he came to be known, turned the play into a 67-yard touchdown. The fans who still remained erupted onto the field, and it took several minutes to clear them away so that Crain could kick the extra point for the 14–13 victory.

It was the Longhorns' first victory in an SWC opener since 1933, and in Bible's words, "That play and that victory changed our outlook—mine, the players', the student body's, and the ex-students'. Things had been going pretty badly up until that game. The way was still long, but we had tasted the fruits of victory, and we were on our way."

The 1938 freshmen didn't get off to the best of starts. The Longhorns were 1–8 for the year, which included a 14–3 loss to Baylor.

The Immortal 13

They called it "The Impossible Catch." Noble Doss hauls in an over-the-shoulder, 32-yard pass that carried Texas to the Texas A&M one-yard line. Doss also set a school record with three pass interceptions in this game.

From the time D. X. Bible had become the Texas football coach in 1937, the Longhorns had flirted with excellence. There were a few great moments and even some good games, but Bible's Longhorns still hadn't faced the challenge they were about to meet on Thanksgiving Day of 1940.

Since the opening of Memorial Stadium in 1924, Texas had never lost to Texas A&M in Austin. But the Aggie team that came calling that Turkey Day was formidable, having claimed the national championship the year before. With hopes of a second straight title and a trip to the Rose Bowl, the Aggies came into Austin riding a 19-game unbeaten streak. Texas was a respectable 6–2 on the season, with Southwest Conference losses to Rice and SMU. Confident Aggie fans were among the 45,000 who jammed the stadium.

Texas had survived the Aggie challenge in Austin in the down years of 1936 and 1938, but when Coach Homer Norton brought his team—led by All-Americans John Kimbrough at fullback and Marshall Robnett at guard—into the stadium, stopping this juggernaut seemed all but impossible. But Bible, a master of motivation as well as football fundamentals, had his team ready. The festive holiday crowd was jolted out of their seats by a Longhorn touchdown in the first 57 seconds of play.

Texas started the 65-yard drive with a throwback pass from Pete Layden to Jack Crain for 32 yards. Two snaps later, Noble Doss made a twisting, over-the-head catch that took him out of bounds at the Aggie one-yard line. Behind blocking by Julian Garrett, Chal Daniel, and Vernon Martin, Layden scored on the next play, and Crain kicked the extra point for a 7–0 lead. Although 59 minutes remained, Texas had recorded the only score in what became a crushing 7–0 defeat of perhaps the greatest team in Aggie history.

On this cool, cloudy day in an era when players played both offense and defense, Texas fielded only 13 men—9 of whom played the game's entire 60 minutes. They became known as "The Immortal 13."

Bible's Poetry Reading

Texas's shocking 7–0 defeat of the defending national champions has gone down as one of the most memorable moments in the Longhorns' first 50 years of football. Players credited the victory to an inspirational poem. Passing out copies of Edgar Guest's "It Couldn't Be Done" so the team could follow along, Coach Bible read it to them just before they took the field:

Somebody said that it couldn't be done,
  But he with a chuckle replied
That "maybe it couldn't," but he would be one
  Who wouldn't say so till he'd tried.
So he buckled right in with the trace of a grin
  On his face. If he worried he hid it.
He started to sing as he tackled the thing
  That couldn't be done, and he did it.
Somebody scoffed: "Oh, you'll never do that;
  At least no one ever has done it";
But he took off his coat and he took off his hat,
  And the first thing we knew he'd begun it.
With a lift of his chin and a bit of a grin,
  Without any doubting or quiddit,
He started to sing as he tackled the thing
  That couldn't be done, and he did it.
There are thousands to tell you it cannot be done,
  There are thousands to prophesy failure;
There are thousands to point out to you one by one,
  The dangers that wait to assail you.
But just buckle in with a bit of a grin,
  Just take off your coat and go to it;
Just start in to sing as you tackle the thing
  That "cannot be done," and you'll do it.

Dreams of Roses

One of D. X. Bible's promises when he started in 1937 was to have a winner in five years. As the 1941 season approached, it appeared that he was right on target. From the 1940 team that finished 8–2, Bible saw 18 returning lettermen, 16 of them seniors and 9 from the squad that had defeated Texas A&M.

Before the season, Wilbur Evans wrote in the *Austin American-Statesman*, "Bible admits his personnel leaves little to be desired. Talent runs so deep that sophomores are going to have a hard time landing anything better than a second-team slot. And even that honor is going to be rough to attain."

Preseason rankings had UT as the odds-on favorite to win the Southwest Conference, and the few national rankings of the time had Texas well up in the Top 10. Football in the Southwest had earned respect: SMU, TCU, and Texas A&M had won national championships in 1935, 1938, and 1939, respectively. Returning seniors Noble Doss, Jack Crain, and Pete Layden were joined by Spec Sanders, a superb junior college transfer. The offense was potent, scoring at least 34 points in each of its first six games. In that same window, Texas posted three shutouts and had given up only 27 points—14 of which came in a 48–14 shellacking of Arkansas.

The first challenge of the season was expected to come against Rice in the fifth game, but Texas pounded the Owls 40–0. Suddenly Texas sat atop the Associated Press national rankings in a tie with Minnesota. Just ahead on the schedule was a road trip to Dallas to face

SMU, a team the Longhorns hadn't beaten since 1933. In fact, they hadn't even scored a touchdown in Dallas since then.

The Texas offense was adequate, posting its 34 points, but the defense was superb, shutting out the Mustangs. After the game, SMU coach Matty Bell called Texas "the greatest team in Southwest Conference history," a group that included his own national champs of 1935. "I didn't have but 16 men," Bell said. "D. X. has three full teams."

When the team returned from Dallas and gathered in the Hill Hall dining room for the team meal, there was a long-stemmed red rose at every plate. "This is for the Rose Bowl, because that is where you're going," housemother Mrs. J. M. Griffith, better known as "Miz Griff," told them.

Texas moved firmly to the No. 1 spot in the AP poll, far outdistancing Minnesota. And *Life* magazine sent photog-

It's easy to display your allegiance with a Texas pin on your jacket lapel.

Texas's 1941 team rose to No. 1 in the nation midway through the season. Here the team poses with their mascot, Bevo.

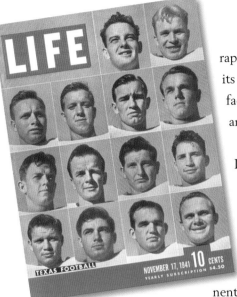

Long before Sports Illustrated or other well-known national magazines devoted entirely to sports, the appearance of a football team in a national weekly newsmagazine was a rarity.

raphers to put the team on the front of its November 17 issue, immortalizing the faces of 14 Longhorns with the cover and an eight-page spread.

But the SMU win had taken its toll. Layden had left the game with a hurt ankle, Doss injured an arm and came up with an infected toe during the next week, and Malcolm Kutner ruptured a blood vessel in an elbow.

Baylor, the Longhorns' next opponent, had lost its last four games, including a 48–0 shutout to Texas A&M. A crowd of only 12,000 was present in Waco to see what was expected to be a runaway. But Texas didn't face just a stumbling block; it hit a brick wall. The limping Longhorns held a late 7–0 lead when Baylor scored with less than 30 seconds remaining to tie the game for good at 7–7.

Texas dropped to second behind Minnesota in the AP poll, but it still was on track for a chance at the championship and the Rose Bowl. The disconsolate Longhorns, however, lost to TCU 14–7 the next week.

Not yet out for the count, Texas rebounded in the following game with a 23–0 victory over Texas A&M at Kyle Field in College Station. With only a nonconference game against Oregon remaining, the Longhorns—who had never before been to a bowl game—rekindled hopes for a trip to Pasadena and the Rose Bowl. The problem they faced, however, was that the Rose Bowl had already invited Oregon State, which had edged Oregon 12–7. While waiting and hoping for a bid from the folks in California, Texas had turned down a bid from the Orange Bowl and declined a chance at the Sugar Bowl. Some officials urged Bible to cancel the game with Oregon to calm the nervous Rose Bowl

committee, but—ever the man of integrity—he refused, citing the principle of holding to a contract as his reason.

The Rose Bowl ultimately invited Duke, and Texas defeated Oregon 71–7 on December 6, 1941. The greatest Texas team of its era finished its season 8–1–1.

As it turned out, the Longhorns would never have made it to California, anyway. The day after the Oregon blowout, the Japanese bombed Pearl Harbor. For that season only, the Rose Bowl was moved for security reasons to Duke's home of Durham, North Carolina.

Red Candles

There is no greater legend of mystic power in Texas history than the story of the Red Candles.

In 1941, Texas's hopes of a national championship had been shattered by a tie to Baylor and a loss to TCU. Coming off the TCU disappointment, the even larger jinx of playing Texas A&M on Kyle Field in College Station was looming.

Ever since the construction of Memorial Stadium and Kyle Field in the 1920s, the home team had always prevailed in this series of arch rivals. And so it was that a group of UT students went to see an Austin fortune-teller named Mrs. Augusta Hipple to ask for a solution to their problem. "Burn red candles," she told them.

Throughout the campus and the city, flames ignited. Longhorn supporters bought every red candle in town, and orders went out for more. And on Thanksgiving Day, Texas defeated Texas A&M 23–0, and the Kyle Field jinx was broken.

In later years, UT supporters would suggest red candles as the solution to a jinx, and most of the time they worked. *Time* magazine called the candles "the most potent whammy in Texas tradition, and nothing to be lightly invoked."

During the 1980s, when environmentalists forced the halt of a bonfire in Austin for the Longhorns, the faithful turned to a midnight "Hex Rally," where red candles were again featured.

The War

It was a typical reaction that Sunday morning. Bob Rochs, who later became one of the most beloved members of the UT athletics department, was walking along 21st Street on his way home from church when someone yelled out the window of Brackenridge Dorm, "Hey! The Japanese just bombed Pearl Harbor!"

"Where in the hell is Pearl Harbor?" Rochs later recalled thinking.

It was December 7, 1941—the day after the greatest team in Texas history (to that point) had played its last game. The United States was entering World War II. The landscape of college football—like the rest of the nation—was about to change dramatically.

As the '42 season approached, the United States was at war. Draft age was 21 but would soon to drop to 18. While 21 lettermen returned to the Longhorns, most of the older players had already entered the Navy, Marine, or Army Air Force Reserves. Two assistant coaches had enlisted in the Navy itself.

Still, Bible pressed forward, committed to his plan of providing an education—and a great football experience—for the young students in his charge. With a 9–2 record for the year, Bible's team claimed that elusive conference championship. A new agreement with the Cotton Bowl in Dallas required that the SWC champion appear there, so dreams of a trip to the Rose Bowl, the nation's most visible college football venue, were put on hold for 60 or so years. Texas distinguished itself by winning the first bowl game it ever played, defeating nationally No. 5 ranked Georgia Tech 14–7.

By 1943, coaches throughout the country were forced to go with players declared physically unfit for the draft (4-F), underage freshmen, or whatever military trainees were on campus. The Southwest Conference was hard hit—Baylor dropped football entirely for 1943 and 1944.

But '43 did produce Bible's second league title, and the subsequent Cotton Bowl berth ended in a 7–7 tie with a team made up of military stars from Randolph Field in San Antonio. The center on that team, Keifer Marshall, took part in every play of the game. Months later, he was among the survivors of the battle of Iwo Jima.

Stan Mauldin was one of the great linemen in the D. X. Bible era of Texas football. Here he leads running back Roy Dale McKay on a sweep. Mauldin went on to a notable pro career with the Chicago Cardinals.

The Tower Lights

It was an unexpected victory, that 9–6 win over Baylor in Waco in 1937, but it started a tradition that would reflect a symbol of success for the University of Texas. Dana X. Bible's first team won only two games that season, but one of them was a stunning victory over the Bears, who were 6–0 with hopes of a national championship and a Rose Bowl bid.

The Austin campus was undergoing a metamorphosis. "Old Main," the tradition-laden building at the center of what was known as "The Forty Acres," had been torn down and replaced by a 27-story structure that would be known as "The Tower." When the building was completed in 1937, one of the modern additions to it was a series of orange lights placed alternately around the long shaft and the carillon clock tower at the top of the building. Under normal lighting conditions, the white lights formed a beacon to the Texas Hill Country—the Tower and the State Capitol were the two tallest buildings in the area. But the orange lights were never intended for normal lighting conditions. In a state where football has always been king, those lights were set to shine when Texas claimed a football victory. In the original plan, the top lights would be turned on for any regular season football victory, except for a win over Texas A&M. That honor would call for the entire shaft to be bathed in orange lights.

So when the Longhorn football team returned on November 6, 1937, after their victory over the No. 4 ranked Bears, they saw the top of the Tower lit orange in celebration of a football victory for the first time ever.

As the years have passed, other sports and other accomplishments have been included in the Tower tribute of lights. When the Longhorn football team won its first national championship in 1963, workers spent several days going room to room and floor to floor, covering windows so that a number *1* could be shown on the orange Tower. The lights also came to be used for Southwest Conference championships in other sports, and by the time Texas won back-to-back national titles in football in 1969 and 1970, shades had been installed on the windows to allow for a quick turnaround of the number *1*.

Academic accomplishments and other significant events are also recognized today, and the lights can accommodate about eight different patterns of tributes. With so many teams in so many sports and other activities, as well, the university now keeps a calendar on its Web site to explain the reasons for the various lighting patterns.

It glows orange with victories. . . . Texas's 27-story main building is known as "The Tower," and beginning in 1937 it has carried the tradition of orange lights at the top after a regular-season UT win.

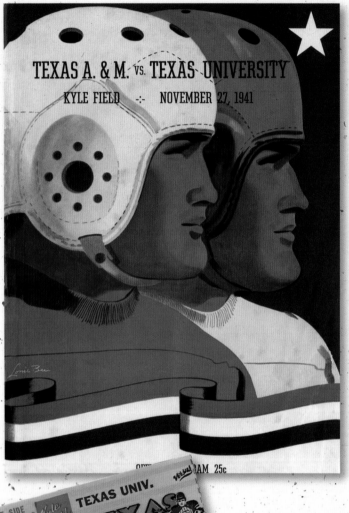

TEXAS A. & M. VS. TEXAS UNIVERSITY

KYLE FIELD -:- NOVEMBER 27, 1941

Perhaps spurred on by red candles, the 1941 Longhorns were the first to defeat the Aggies at home at Kyle Field in College Station. In fact, Texas held A&M scoreless, winning 23–0.

Texas lost its No. 6 ranking after it fell 14–0 to TCU in 1946. The team did better against A&M the next week, winning 24–7, and ended the year at No. 15.

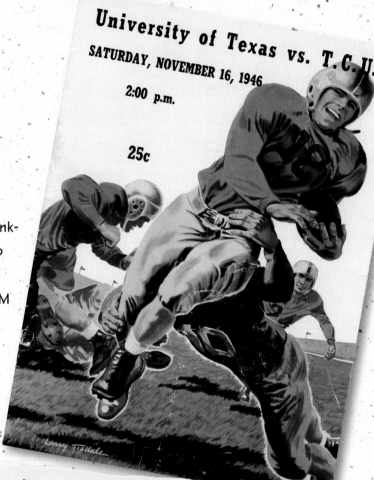

University of Texas vs. T.C.U.

SATURDAY, NOVEMBER 16, 1946

2:00 p.m.

25c

The No. 5 Longhorns won this 1947 game against Texas A&M 32–13, en route to a 10–1 season that included a win over Alabama in the Sugar Bowl. First-year coach Blair Cherry missed the Thanksgiving Day game after undergoing emergency appendectomy surgery the previous Friday.

First Time's the Charm
Friday, January 1, 1943
Longhorns Cage Bulldogs 14–7

Although the University of Texas had never appeared in a postseason bowl game before, after an 8–2 season and a Southwest Conference championship, they certainly seemed to know their way around the Cotton Bowl. Led by backs Roy Dale McKay and Jackie Field, the Longhorns proved all the naysayers wrong who believed they couldn't compete with the University of Georgia Bulldogs.

This All-American helmet was worn by Louis "Bud" McFadin, named an All-American in both 1949 and 1950. An offensive guard and defensive tackle, he was the Southwest Conference's Most Valuable Player in 1950 and was a first-round draft pick for the Los Angeles Rams.

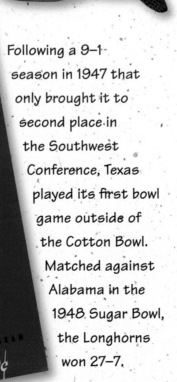

SUGAR BOWL

TULANE SUGAR BOWL STADIUM

NEW ORLEANS

Jan. 1 1948

14TH ANNUAL CLASSIC

SOUVENIR PROGRAM

ALABAMA vs. TEXAS

50¢

Following a 9–1 season in 1947 that only brought it to second place in the Southwest Conference, Texas played its first bowl game outside of the Cotton Bowl. Matched against Alabama in the 1948 Sugar Bowl, the Longhorns won 27–7.

Cheerleaders were excited by the matchup in the 1949 Orange Bowl. Texas again placed second in the Southwest Conference and accepted a bid to meet the No. 8 Georgia Bulldogs, whom they handily defeated 41–28.

The Legend of Bobby Layne

Bobby Layne and Hub Bechtol would turn into an All-American pass-catch tandem for the Longhorns of the post–World War II era. Here, Bechtol takes a pass from Layne in the 1946 Cotton Bowl victory over Missouri. Both would later be inducted into the National Football Foundation College Football Hall of Fame.

Few players in the first 75 years of college football matched the freewheeling, touchdown-scoring, hell-raising, lovable nature of Bobby Layne.

Layne had come to the University of Texas as a recruit for baseball, but it didn't take long for D. X. Bible to see that the blonde young man from Dallas had a rare gift. Layne helped lead Texas to a 5–4 record in 1944 before entering the merchant marine and missing part of the season of 1945.

In that year, the Longhorns had suffered only one loss, 7–6 to Rice, when Layne was released from the merchant marine at the end of World War II. Rejoining his teammates, Layne led Texas to a 12–7 victory over the SMU Mustangs. Victories over Baylor, TCU, and Texas A&M followed, and with a 9–1 record, Texas was on its way to the Cotton Bowl.

That's where Layne would begin to construct his legend. The first part of that legend cast Layne as a free spirit. As the Longhorns prepared for their bowl game against Missouri, Layne and his friend Rooster Andrews met some of the Missouri players at lunch.

"Those Missouri guys were a good bunch," Layne recalled. "We got to visiting at the luncheon, so I told Rooster to invite some of them over to our hotel that night for a little party. Nothing wild, mind you. Just some light refreshments and a good bull session. They headed back to their hotel well before curfew."

The next day, Layne cemented his legend. He accounted for every Longhorn point in a 40–27 victory: He ran for three touchdowns, caught a 50-yard pass for another, completed passes for the other two, and kicked four extra points. He completed 11 of 12 passes

Few players in UT history have captured the imagination of Longhorn fans as did Bobby Layne, who became Texas's first All-American quarterback in 1947. His larger-than-life image was enhanced by stories of his competitiveness and his "good ole boy" antics.

BECHTOL

for 158 yards. The only incompletion he tallied was a pass dropped by a receiver in the fourth quarter.

Layne would go on to become one of the greatest baseball players in Texas history as well. As a pitcher, he was 28–0 in Southwest Conference games, including a no-hitter at Texas A&M when he was playing with a severely cut foot—the pain of which he masked when Andrews sneaked a six-pack of beer into a hidden area behind the UT bench.

When Layne left Texas, he owned every passing record in school history, and though time and evolving offenses have toppled most of them, 60 years after his final season, Layne was still second in all-time quarterback wins for the Longhorns with 28.

The 1946 season was bittersweet for Layne and his teammates. Early in the season, Texas was rolling. The Longhorns opened the year against Missouri, the team they had beaten in the Cotton Bowl, and hammered the Tigers 42–0. A 76–0 victory over Colorado and a 54–6 win over highly regarded Oklahoma A&M vaulted Texas to No. 1 in the country. The only losses were an 18–13 defeat at Rice and a 14–0 shutout at TCU. But those losses denied Texas a conference championship, despite an 8–2 season.

Bible, who had decided to retire after the season, rejected overtures for an Orange Bowl bid for his team. His ten-year record was 63–31–3, with three Southwest Conference titles.

Layne adapted well to the new *T* formation of Blair Cherry, who was elevated to head coach for the 1947 season. With Layne flourishing as a true quarterback for the first time after Bible's single-wing days, he followed a 10–1 season in his senior year of 1947 by taking Texas to a 27–7 victory over Alabama in the Sugar Bowl.

Rooster Andrews

He stood barely five feet tall, but in the annals of Texas football history, he was a giant. Billy Andrews had entered the University of Texas in 1941, and he worked part-time cleaning Gregory Gymnasium's basketball arena and as a student manager for the football team.

It was during his freshman season that he gained the nickname that became as much a part of Texas Longhorn history as "Bevo." A group of football players had championed a rooster in rural "chicken fights," and it lived in a tree. Once when the rooster had moved to the top and refused to come down, the players needed Billy to climb up to get it: Billy Andrews was the only guy small enough to climb the tree. He got the rooster, but he fell and broke his arm in the effort. Forever after that, he was known as "Rooster" Andrews.

Rooster would also become known as the All-America water boy. Deemed too small to enter the service in World War II, he served as the team manager, but he actually got some on-the-field play. He once drop-kicked an extra point and scored on an extra-point conversion pass.

Rooster went into the sporting goods business, and for more than 50 years, he served as one of the best goodwill ambassadors Texas ever had.

After his Texas career, Layne played 15 years in the NFL, reuniting with high school friend, SMU rival, and fellow merchant marine Doak Walker to win two world championships with the Detroit Lions. Before he died of a heart attack in 1986 at age 59, Layne had been inducted into the NFL Hall of Fame and the Texas Longhorn Hall of Honor.

Blair Cherry

The popular Cherry was head coach for only four seasons. He later attributed his abrupt departure to criticism and pressure from "some uninformed and careless sports writers who made my job continually more difficult."

Joining D. X. Bible's Texas Longhorns staff in 1937, Blair Cherry had waited a long time for his chance at the top position. He'd already had a successful coaching career in high school football, taking over the Amarillo team in 1930 and leading it to an incredible record of 84 wins against only 5 losses. Amarillo was the state champion for each of Cherry's final three years there. When Texas was looking for new leadership in 1937, they considered Cherry, but he was ultimately second choice to Bible.

Bible saw Cherry's talent and brought him on board, and Cherry stepped into his position as Bible's right-hand man. When Bible resigned as coach after the '46 season, he retained his position as athletics director, and it was in that capacity that he handpicked Cherry to take his place as coach. It didn't take long for Cherry, the Longhorns'

first Texas-born coach, to demonstrate why he'd been in contention for the top job a decade earlier.

All-America quarterback Bobby Layne led a veteran squad of Longhorns in 1947, and under Cherry's guiding hand, the team posted a near-perfect record of 10–1, losing only a classic 14–13 battle against Doak Walker and SMU. That took Texas to the Sugar Bowl, where No. 6 Alabama went down to defeat. The Longhorns finished Cherry's first season ranked fifth in the nation.

Success continued, and Cherry's 1948 team had a record of 7–3–1, which included a 41–28 Orange Bowl victory over No. 8 Georgia. That triumph caught the eye of some professional teams, and both the Chicago Cardinals and the Washington Redskins of the NFL offered Cherry their head coaching positions, but the Texas native preferred to stay at the university, where he accepted a new five-year contract.

But in only the second year of that agreement, Cherry announced that he was leaving his position to go into private business. The 1949 Longhorns had produced a winning 6–4 record, and the 1950 team was doing even better: On their way to a final ranking of No. 3 based on a 9–2 record, the Longhorns went undefeated, 6–0, in conference play to claim the Southwest Conference championship. But Cherry suffered from an ulcer and insomnia, and he explained himself the next year in a *Saturday Evening Post* article entitled, "Why I Quit Coaching." An "over-emphasis on winning," along with media and fan criticism he received over the few losses in his incredible 32–10–1 Longhorn career were the reasons he gave for leaving. Although his Texas head coaching career lasted only four seasons, Cherry is remembered as one of the best leaders the Longhorns have ever seen.

Capping an excellent first year as head coach, Blair Cherry took his 5th-ranked Longhorns to a 27–7 New Year's Day win over the 6th-ranked Alabama Crimson Tide in the 1948 Sugar Bowl.

Ed Price

Shocked by Cherry's sudden resignation, the university moved quickly to fill the head coaching position with longtime assistant Edwin Booth Price, who had spent even more time on the Texas Longhorn staff than Blair Cherry. Price had joined the football staff in 1936, a year before Cherry, and had served as an assistant under three coaches—Jack Chevigny, D. X. Bible, and Cherry himself. He was an obvious choice to step into Cherry's shoes for the '51 season.

Price's first season as head coach was another winner, as the Longhorns went 7–3. They improved on that in 1952, taking the Southwest Conference championship title with an unbeaten 6–0 record in conference play and earning an overall record of 9–2. With an all-conference backfield, Texas ended the season ranked No. 10 nationally. The Longhorns finished their winning ways that season by shutting out Tennessee, No. 8 nationally, 16–0 in the Cotton Bowl.

In 1953, Price continued coaching the team to a championship level of play, finishing with a 7–3 record and a national ranking of 11, although the Longhorns had to settle for a league cochampionship. With two conference titles in three years and a winning record of 23–8, there was no reason to believe that the good times wouldn't continue.

But in 1954, unfortunately, those good times disappeared. Texas struggled to a 4–5–1 season—the first losing record the Longhorns had experienced in 16 years. And this was only the beginning. The team did a bit better in 1955, battling to a .500 record with five wins and losses, but if that seemed to be a turn of the tide, everything fell apart the next year. In 1956, the Longhorns compiled the worst record UT has ever experienced even to this day: 1–9. The only item in the win column was the season's second game, a 7–6 contest against Tulane.

Price insisted that the Longhorns' misfortune was the result of academic rule changes at the university, but some argued that Price wasn't tough enough and that his recruiting had not been up to snuff. Either way, midway through the schedule on October 31, 1956, Price offered his resignation, to take effect when the season ended. As a student, he had played for Texas and been a sportswriter for the *Daily Texan*. In his professional career, he had been part of the UT athletic staff for more than 20 years. No one doubted it when he said his decision had been made "for the good of the team." Price remained at Texas, teaching in the physical education department and then serving for a number of years as an assistant dean of students.

One of the most respected men in Texas athletic history, Ed Price, seen here in a Murray Olderman cartoon, moved from coaching into university administration, were he stayed until his retirement in the 1960s.

Memories of 1955

The autumn of 1955 was not spectacular for the University of Texas on the gridiron, but in terms of history, the year produced two of the best-known symbols of Longhorn lore.

Up north, the University of Chicago had given up its football program, so a Texas benefactor named D. Harold Byrd went there and purchased a giant bass drum, which he then donated to the UT Longhorn Band. The drum, eight feet in diameter and weighing more than 500 pounds, became known as "Big Bertha" and was labeled "the world's biggest drum." It has been part of the band's performances ever since.

The second innovation of '55 became even bigger than the band and the drum.

In the second-to-last game of the season, Texas was getting ready to host TCU, which at that time was a power in the Southwest Conference. The Longhorn faithful were preparing for a pep rally the night before the game when cheerleader Harley Clark and his friend Henry Pitts were playing around with shadow signs cast on a blank dorm wall. Pitts discovered that if he extended his index finger and little finger and tucked down his middle and ring fingers with his thumb, he could form something that looked like a steer's head.

Hand signals were nothing new. After all, Longhorns' rival Texas A&M had used a "thumbs-up" sign and a cry of "gig 'em" as part of its battle attack for years. So at the pep rally the night before the TCU game, Clark showed the enthusiastic student audience the new steer sign, accompanying it with the words, "Hook 'em, Horns!"

Although it didn't seem to help the next day—TCU crushed Texas—the tradition was born. Fans in the stands flashed the sign, and that was only the beginning. Clark went on to get a law degree at Texas, and he later became a state district judge. The sign he created became recognized throughout the country and, for that matter, around the world as a symbol of the University of Texas.

When Mack Brown was hired to coach at Texas in 1998, he quickly learned the importance of the salute. "In Texas," he said, "you don't have to say 'hello' . . . you just say 'hook 'em!'"

"Big Bertha" is a fixture for the band at everything from football games to U.S. presidential inaugural parades.

The Tower looks out over Texas Memorial Stadium and the University of Texas campus on a beautiful Austin day.

OFFICIAL PROGRAM • TWENTY-FIVE CENTS

TEXAS vs UNIVERSITY OF IDAHO

MEMORIAL STADIUM

OCTOBER 1, 1949

The Longhorns demolished Idaho 56–7 in 1949. As a result, the previously unranked team rose to No. 12 nationally.

In this ad, which appeared in national magazines, Texaco proudly shows off its contribution to the renovation of Texas Memorial Stadium. The new additions made room for approximately 20,000 more Longhorn fans.

University of Texas enlarges its stadium

Access streets, parking areas, sidewalks, area under stands are paved with Texaco Asphaltic Concrete

The enlarged stadium of the University of Texas. Photo taken during game with Louisiana State University. General contractor was R. P. Farnsworth Company, Inc., of Houston. Texaco Asphalt paving was laid by Collins Construction Company, Austin.

Laying 2-inch Texaco Asphaltic Concrete paving on one of the streets leading to the stadium.

Under the stands, the 1½-inch asphalt surface was laid on a crushed stone base.

A Texaco Asphaltic Concrete sidewalk 15 to 20 feet wide was laid around most of the stadium.

The University of Texas has increased the seating capacity of its stadium from 46,000 to 66,000 at a cost of $1,400,000.

An interesting feature of this noteworthy project is the variety of service which resilient, joint-free Texaco Asphalt paving is called upon to perform. In addition to several streets leading to the stadium, Texaco Asphaltic Concrete paving of the hot-mix, hot-laid type was laid on sidewalks and parking areas, as well as the area underneath the seats. A 2-inch asphalt surface was specified for the streets, while 1½ inches was considered adequate elsewhere.

Texaco Asphalt Cements, Cutback Asphalts and Slow-curing Asphaltic Oils meet every construction and maintenance need of the road builder. Refined from carefully selected crudes, these products are backed by 45 years of successful performance on America's streets and highways.

Two helpful booklets which describe all types of asphalt road and street construction may be obtained without charge by writing our nearest office.

THE TEXAS COMPANY, Asphalt Sales Dept., 135 E. 42nd Street, New York City 17
Boston 16   Chicago 4   Denver 1   Houston 1   Jacksonville 2   Philadelphia 2   Richmond 19

TEXACO ASPHALT

The largest crowd of its era—67,600 fans—packed Texas Memorial Stadium in 1952 when the Longhorns played the Fighting Irish of Notre Dame. The 19th-ranked Irish upset the 5th-ranked Longhorns 14–3 as Irish coach Frank Leahy exhorted his troops to a comeback by telling them, "You're not playing like Notre Dame men. Go out there and play like Notre Dame men."

Texas appeared in the Sugar Bowl only once from 1937 through 1956, defeating Alabama 27–7 in 1948.

The Longhorn Band, the Showband of the Southwest, has long been an important part of the Texas football experience. These tubas, pictured from 1955, demonstrate the band's focus on pride and spirit.

It was time for revenge when Texas played Tennessee in the 1953 Cotton Bowl following the 1952 season. The Vols had upset the Longhorns 20–14 following the 1950 season. This time, Texas pitched a shutout, winning 16–0.

TEXAS A&M Game
AUSTIN • NOVEMBER 25, 1954
Official Program • 25¢

Program covers with popular art charmed Texas Longhorn fans for almost a quarter of a century. Here for the 1954 Texas A&M game, the artist plays on Texas domination of the series in Austin. Again, the Horns prevailed, winning 22–13 despite finishing the season with a 4–5–1 record.

The Royal Years

1957–1976

The Longhorns had fallen off their stride in the middle 1950s, and something had to be done to bring the team back to the winning records the university, its students, and its alumni had become accustomed to. Although they didn't know it at the time, Texas was about to encounter the coach who would hold the reins on the team longer than any other.

The showdown of the 1963 season came when the No. 2 Longhorns met the No. 1 Oklahoma Sooners for bragging rights in a Red River shootout that had national title implications.

Opposite: *Darrell Royal and his Long-horns wait for the coin flip prior to a meeting with the Oklahoma Sooners during the early 1960s at the Cotton Bowl stadium in Dallas. The pose, crouched on one knee, would become familiar to fans and media who saw Royal as one of the keenest observers and "game day" coaches of his time.*

Beginning the Royal Era

Darrell Royal has been honored by his alma mater Oklahoma and by Texas. Here Royal (21), who still holds several Sooner records, runs past Longhorn Spot Collins (65) in 1946's Texas-OU match.

It was a long list, and his name wasn't on it. The University of Texas was looking for a new head football coach, and a whole lot of people wanted the job. To a young Darrell Royal in faraway Seattle, Washington, the leap of faith seemed almost as far as the distance in miles.

Royal had grown up in Hollis, Oklahoma, just across the Red River from the state of Texas. He had played football at OU, and once, when he and his wife, Edith, were driving through Austin, he commented that it "sure would be nice to one day coach at the University of Texas."

But if the distance itself weren't difficult enough already, the timing seemed impossible. Royal had started his head coaching career in Canada, and he had coached two seasons at Mississippi State before taking the job at the Univer-sity of Washington in 1956. His Huskies team had broken even at 5–5 that season.

Longhorns have always dreamed big, and this search committee was no exception. The highest profile names in the college game were on the list of candidates: Frank Leahy at Notre Dame, Murray Warmath at Minnesota, Bobby Dodd at Georgia Tech, Duffy Daugherty at Michigan State. Texas made a run at each of them, all to no avail.

So when the quest for the "big name" failed, Athletics Director D. X. Bible and his committee decided to re-direct the search toward a young, vibrant coach who was yet to be discovered. They went back to their original list and started asking the candidates for suggestions. Separately and simultaneously, Dodd and Daugherty offered the same name: Darrell Royal.

Bible invited Royal to come for an interview, and Royal quickly began studying the committee members and their history. By the time he got to Austin, he knew not only their names but what they did and who they were married to. He also impressed the committee with a maturity, an understanding, and a competitive zeal that seemed unusual for someone of 32 years.

Royal's character and values had been forged by the skin-cutting winds of Dust Bowl Oklahoma—landscape that had once been good farming country but was no longer, as epitomized in John Steinbeck's *The Grapes of Wrath*. As a young man, Royal had gone west with his family, looking for work like so many others whose lives had been uprooted by drought and the Great Depression.

Football had been his ticket to a different life. First, he had hitchhiked back to Hollis from California to play high

who would direct the Texas defense during Royal's 20 years, and four men who would successfully go on to become head coaches themselves elsewhere—Jim Pittman (Tulane and TCU), Charley Shira (Mississippi State), Jack Swarthout (Montana), and Ray Willsey (California).

Despite Royal's assessment that a coach who comes in following a 1–9 season (as the Longhorns had earned in 1956) "doesn't inherit a warm bed," his first team at Texas finished with a surprising 6–3–1 record and a berth in the Sugar Bowl against a powerful Ole Miss program. Included in the season was a stunning 9–7 victory at College Station over a highly regarded

At 32, Royal was the country's youngest coach when he took the Texas job. Shown here at practice with one of his first Texas teams, Royal became the winningest coach in the history of the Southwest Conference.

school ball. His college career was delayed by service in World War II, but when he took to the field again, it was at the University of Oklahoma, where he became a star for Hall of Fame coach Bud Wilkinson.

When he took the Texas job in December 1956, Darrell Royal was the youngest head coach in America. Royal retained two members of the previous coaching group, T Jones and Bob Schulze, for his first staff. The rest of the staff he assembled was new and included Mike Campbell,

Texas A&M club led by Heisman Trophy winner John David Crow.

The Sugar Bowl game, however, didn't end as Royal would have wanted. Ole Miss trounced Texas 39–7, and Royal was so disgusted with his team's performance that he gave away his bowl watch to a stranger on the streets of New Orleans. In his time, however, Royal would become the winningest coach in school history and would take his teams to 16 bowl games in 20 years.

Tilling the Soil: Royal's Legend Begins

In the beginning, there were two missions for Darrell Royal at Texas, and it was impossible to assess the order in which they should be addressed. One task was getting the Longhorns back into the race for the Southwest Conference championship. The other, just as pressing, was ending the domination the Oklahoma Sooners had inflicted on the Longhorns during the 1950s. Of course, Texas wasn't alone in that experience. Royal's old coach, Bud Wilkinson, had established the premier football program in the country. True, by the time the Longhorns of 1958 headed to Dallas to face them, the Sooners had won six straight games in the annual battle at the Texas State Fair—but OU had also reeled off an NCAA-record 47 straight victories until Notre Dame had stopped them in 1957. For Royal, the games against his old school would become the benchmark gauge of national respect.

"The only way anybody's going to beat Oklahoma is go out there and whip 'em, jaw to jaw," he said on the Wednesday before the game. "Texas has to develop a football tradition. It had one once but lost it. When we get one, maybe we can stop that bloodletting up at Dallas and turn it into a good show."

The NCAA rules committee had made a significant change in scoring in 1958, changing the point-after-touchdown options to allow one point for a successful kick and two if a team successfully chose to run or pass into the end zone. Royal had been a vocal opponent of the new rule, so it shocked everyone when he used the two-point option successfully after the Longhorns scored first in the game. Oklahoma overcame the 8–0 lead however, and it appeared to be business as usual for the Sooners

until UT quarterback Bobby Lackey hit end Bob Bryant for a seven-yard scoring pass with 3:10 left to play. When Lackey kicked the extra point and the UT defense stopped the Sooners, the Longhorns won 15–14. It was one of the first times in NCAA history that a two-point conversion decided the outcome of a game. Thus began Royal's own domination of the series: Texas won 11 of the next 12 games between the two.

A year later, the Longhorns won their first Southwest Conference championship under Royal, earning a three-way tie with TCU and Arkansas. Because both the Horned Frogs and the Razorbacks had appeared as the league's official representative in the Cotton Bowl more recently than Texas, the 'Horns represented the SWC in a rugged battle

It's a victory ride for Darrell Royal as his 1958 Longhorn team notches a 15–14 victory over Oklahoma in the Cotton Bowl stadium in Dallas.

against No. 1 ranked Syracuse. The Orangemen won 23–14, but the 9–2 record UT posted for the year was its best in almost a decade.

After three years, the Sooners had been disposed of and the stated goal of winning the Southwest Conference had been accomplished. Royal moved on to loftier dreams. With the 1961 season, the quest for national honors became a reality.

Long a disciple of the winged-T offense, Royal employed the first of his innovations that would change the college game. With 21 veterans returning in an era when players played both offense and defense, Royal had tremendous depth. He also had an All-America running back in James Saxton. So Royal devised an offense that would flip the line, end, and wingback to the power of whichever formation they were running. The "flip-flop" met with amazing success. The Longhorns ran three complete teams on offense, and it wasn't until the seventh game of the season that Saxton and other starters had actually played enough to earn a letter. In a time before the high-scoring offenses of two-platoon ball, the 1961 Longhorns defeated their opponents 30–6 on average. When they beat SMU 27–0 in the seventh game of the year, Texas ascended to the No. 1 ranking in the country.

The dream died two weeks later, however. Saxton was injured early in the game, and TCU stunned the Longhorns 6–0. Royal's squad had experienced life at the top, though, and as the next three years would reflect, they liked what they had seen.

The First Bowl Victory

The 1961 Texas season had seen the Longhorns experience a No. 1 national ranking for the first time in 20 years, and while the national championship eluded them, 'Horns fans still had a chance to celebrate at the end of the year. Darrell Royal's first bowl experience in the Sugar Bowl after the 1957 season had been sour, and after a loss in the 1960 Cotton Bowl to Syracuse and a 3–3 tie in the Bluebonnet Bowl the next season, Royal's crew was still looking for its first bowl victory.

When Southwest Conference champ Texas headed to the Cotton Bowl after the 1961 season, it was matched against a strong Ole Miss team just a couple of years removed from a No. 1 ranking. Although their offense had earned most of the accolades that year, the Longhorns won a defensive struggle 12–7. The Longhorns went on to win five of six bowl games they played in the rest of the 1960s for a decade bowl record of 6–1–1.

Triumphing over Tragedy

One of the most famous Texas plays of the early 1960s saw linebackers Johnny Treadwell (60) and Pat Culpepper (31) stop Arkansas running back Danny Brabham at the goal line.

On the first day of September in 1962, the carefree world of the young men of the Southwest Conference came to a screeching halt. The tragedy of life's fragility came hard on the first day of practice for the college teams in Texas.

The temperature was only in the 80s, but coupled with high humidity, it caused players at several schools—and in particular Texas and SMU—to suffer severely. Late in the Longhorns' practice, three Longhorns, including sophomore Reggie Grob, dropped and were hospitalized. Grob never recovered. He died of kidney and liver failure the Monday before the Longhorns' opening game. At SMU, linebacker Mike Kelsey also collapsed on the first day of practice and died the next day.

Grob's teammates attended his funeral on a Friday and opened the season against Mel Renfro and Oregon the next day. This dispiriting atmosphere served as a backdrop for one of the most famous home games in Longhorn history.

As it had the previous season, Texas rose to No. 1 in the rankings, this time after a 9–6 victory over Oklahoma. Next up were the Arkansas Razorbacks, due in Austin for a national showdown. The Razorbacks were ranked seventh nationally, and a crowd in the mid-60,000s jammed Texas Memorial Stadium for the game that clear October night.

The Razorbacks struck first and held a 3–0 lead in the third quarter when the most memorable play of the game—and of the first five years of Darrell Royal's tenure at Texas, for that matter—occurred. Arkansas had driven to the Texas three-yard line and threatened for a touchdown. Razorback fullback Danny Brabham crashed into the line on third down and was met head-on by Texas linebackers Johnny Treadwell and Pat Culpepper. Culpepper pushed his helmet onto the ball and forced it to pop out in the end zone, where Longhorn defensive back Joe Dixon caught it for a recovered fumble, defusing the danger of a Razorbacks score.

In the fourth quarter, Texas drove 85 yards in 20 plays, scoring on a three-yard run by Tommy Ford to win the game 7–3 with only 36 seconds remaining.

Texas Orange and White

When Longhorn coach Mack Brown came to Texas and urged Longhorn nation to, among other things, "wear orange with pride," he had no way of knowing that the subject of his encouragement dated back almost 100 years and had endured both myths and truths along the way.

Texas orange and white had been chosen by a student, faculty, and alumni vote. Of the 1,111 votes cast, 562 were for orange and white, 310 for orange and maroon, and 203, primarily from the medical school, for royal blue.

Royal Takes a Stand

Since coming to Texas in 1957, Darrell Royal had been particularly "fan friendly." At noon on each Wednesday during the season, he met members of the Austin Longhorn Club downtown at the Paramount Theater, where he showed the previous week's game film and offered comments on the upcoming opponent.

But the fans often had critics among them. Texas had beaten Oklahoma 9–6, but for some at the Paramount Theater, that wasn't impressive enough. Royal went on the attack.

"I'm getting damned sick and tired of people asking, 'What's wrong with the Longhorns?'" Royal began. "Out of our last 15 games, we've won 14. People want to know, 'What's wrong with our offense?' They want to know, 'Why did their line whip our line?' Some people think there's only one team in the conference, and that's the University of Arkansas. I can tell you we're not going out there to lose.

"I don't need any suggestions. I don't need any new plays. I'm satisfied with our team and the plays we've got. For that reason, I don't want to throw it open to any questions."

He received a standing ovation. And as he promised, Texas didn't go out against Arkansas to lose.

The orange-and-white combination had been around since 1885, when students looking to show school spirit had—either by choice or chance—settled on ribbons of those colors. In the early days, the orange dye used was a brighter orange that faded when washed, causing some opponents to label the Texas team with the derogatory term of *yellow bellies*. In 1928, football and track coach Clyde Littlefield commissioned the development of a unique color—and the dye to create it. That color was officially known as "Texas orange."

During World War II, the dye, which came from Germany, became unavailable, forcing Texas to return to a brighter color. But when Darrell Royal came aboard as coach, he sought help from Rooster Andrews—who by then had entered the sporting goods business—to recreate Littlefield's "Texas orange." The color returned to Longhorn uniforms in 1962. With it came the myth that Royal had chosen the shade to be deceptive—it was nearly the same color as the football. "What about the road games?" Royal laughed as he put the rumor to rest. "We wear white on the road, and we've been pretty successful there, too."

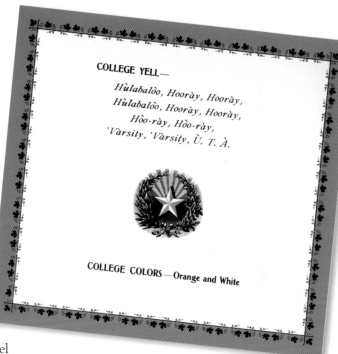

COLLEGE YELL—

Hùlabalòo, Hoorày, Hoorày,
Hùlabalòo, Hoorày, Hoorày,
Hòo-rày, Hòo-rày,
'Vàrsity, 'Vàrsity, Ù. T. À.

COLLEGE COLORS—Orange and White

This print is from an era when the Texas team was known as "Varsity," before a Longhorn steer became the mascot.

Going All the Way

The Grantland Rice Trophy, given by the Football Writers of America, was part of the collection of hardware gathered by the 1963 Longhorns, the university's first team to claim a consensus national championship.

The truth was, Texas had been ever-so-close so many times. But this time, maybe...just maybe...the prognosticators would be right. For two years, Royal's Longhorns had flirted with a chance for their first-ever national championship. Both times the dream eluded them, just as it had since the Associated Press poll began in 1936.

When two national magazines picked the Longhorns as a preseason No. 1, the fall of 1963 seemed a magical time for Texas. Football was the biggest game on campus, and for the University of Texas, the pleasant winds of autumn made everything seem possible.

The Longhorns opened the season with a 21–0 victory over Tulane in New Orleans and quickly vaulted to the No. 2 spot in the country before they headed to Dallas for the annual showdown with No. 1–ranked Oklahoma. Magical times require significant names, and a Hollywood casting agency couldn't have done better than Texas did that year. They had a dashing young quarterback with the gunslinger name of Duke Carlisle and a world-class defense led by a massive tackle named Scott Appleton. In their fourth game of the season, they crushed Oklahoma 28–7 to claim the No. 1 spot in all of college football. Bob Broeg, a sportswriter for the *St. Louis Post-Dispatch*, harkened back to the days of the old West when he summarized the game thusly: "Who's No. 1? It's Texas, pardner. And smile when you say that."

For the next six games, the Longhorns fought off challenger after challenger. The run included a 17–13 win over Arkansas in Little Rock, a 10–6 victory over Rice, and a 17–12 win over SMU. Then, in the biggest

head-on collision in recent Southwest Conference annals, they held off a quality Baylor team 7–0. When Texas put away TCU 17–0 on November 16, it had only to defeat lowly Texas A&M on Thanksgiving Day, November 28, in College Station to win the national championship, which at that time was awarded at the end of the regular season.

The Longhorns were free the weekend between TCU and A&M. On that Friday, November 22, President John F. Kennedy was due to arrive in Austin for a gala dinner. But at 12:30 P.M. in Dallas, President Kennedy was assassinated. Texas Governor John Connally, a loyal Longhorn supporter

End Charles Talbert (89) stands sentinel as he signals "touchdown" for quarterback Duke Carlisle (11), as the Longhorns seal a come-from-behind victory over Texas A&M in the final minutes on a muddy Kyle Field in College Station.

who was with Kennedy, was gravely wounded. Suddenly, a college football game didn't matter much anymore.

The nation froze, glued to television sets for the entire surreal weekend. Vice President Lyndon Baines Johnson, a Texan and a friend of Coach Royal's, assumed the presidency aboard *Air Force One* as the stunned delegation returned to Washington. All college games were canceled; America was in mourning. Officials from Texas and Texas A&M considered canceling the Thanksgiving Day game, as well. Tradition, however, was ultimately deemed an important part of moving the nation forward, and the game went on as scheduled.

Texas A&M had won only twice that season, and Texas was 9–0, so on paper the game was a mismatch. But football isn't played on paper. In fact, this game was played on a sloppy, muddy field—almost a quagmire. Royal and UT Regent Frank Erwin vehemently protested the field conditions, which had been aggravated when extra dirt was mixed with already dead grass. Rain and green dye (for television effect) had turned the field into slush.

The Aggies were making a spirited upset bid, leading the Longhorns 13–3 for much of the game. But in a remarkable finish, UT came from behind to score with just over a minute to play, pulling out a 15–13 win. After the game, Royal spoke by telephone with Connally, who was still in a Dallas hospital. Royal and his captains—Tommy Ford, David McWilliams, and Scott Appleton—went to New York to accept the MacArthur Bowl trophy from the National Football Foundation and Hall of Fame. It was presented by General Douglas MacArthur himself.

Texas had earned its first national championship, but to validate it, the 'Horns had a date with once-beaten Navy and their Heisman Trophy–winning quarterback Roger Staubach in the Cotton Bowl Classic.

Best in the Nation

The Longhorn victory over Texas A&M had clinched the national championship, but it took a 28–6 victory over Roger Staubach and Navy in the Cotton Bowl to silence critics in the Eastern press. Navy, which had lost only to SMU coming into the bowl game, had challenged the Longhorns' claim to the title and were lobbying for a reconsideration. Navy Coach Wayne Hardin even carried the fight to a pregame interview broadcast on national television to 75,000 fans in the Cotton Bowl Stadium.

"When the challenger meets the champion, and the challenger wins, then there is a new champion," Hardin said. The TV commentator then turned the microphone to Royal.

"We're ready," was all that he said.

And he was right. Texas proved it was, indeed, No. 1. Due to Longhorn sacks *(below)*, Staubach finished the game with fewer yards rushing than when he started it: –47 yards on 12 carries. After the game Hardin said, "I've never seen a team which deserved to be No. 1 more than Texas."

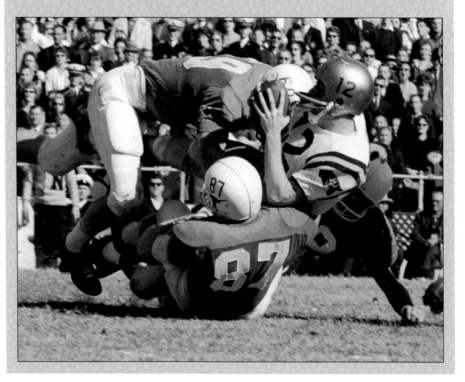

24th ANNUAL COTTON BOWL CLASSIC

Texas vs. Syracuse · Dallas, Texas · January 1, 1960   50¢

Texas took its SWC championship and No. 4 ranking into the 1960 Cotton Bowl against No. 1 Syracuse. The Orangemen won the day by a score of 23–14.

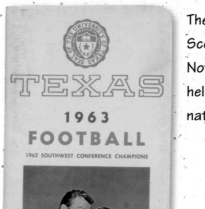

TEXAS 1963 FOOTBALL

1962 SOUTHWEST CONFERENCE CHAMPIONS

Coach Darrell Royal with his All-America Tackle Candidate, Scott Appleton.

The 1963 Media Guide correctly highlighted Scott Appleton as a potential All-American. Not only did he win that honor, but he helped the Longhorns to their first-ever national championship.

The Longhorn Band, directed by Vincent R. Di Nino, proved it was the Show Band of the Southwest with songs such as "The Eyes of Texas," "Texas Taps," and "The Star-Spangled Banner."

The game ball from 1961's match-up with Oklahoma reveals everything we need to know.

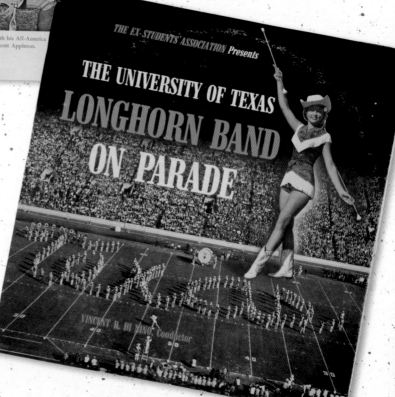

THE EX-STUDENTS' ASSOCIATION Presents

THE UNIVERSITY OF TEXAS LONGHORN BAND ON PARADE

VINCENT R. DI NINO, Conductor

Texas boosters celebrated the team's first national championship in any way they could, including this license plate.

A championship ring is among the most prized possessions a college football player can attain. The 1963 Longhorns wore theirs with pride.

Postcards such as this allowed Longhorns to send their good news to all their friends.

Darrell Royal and his 1963 coaching staff got their share of commemorations, as well. Every glass of water could be a reminder of how Texas had dominated in 1963.

It wasn't an exact replica of Texas Memorial Stadium, but this ashtray was one more method of celebrating the Longhorns' accomplishment.

Tommy Nobis Takes on Joe Namath

Tommy Nobis (60) was arguably the greatest defensive player in UT history. He was also a very good offensive guard, but his rock-solid defense earned him the Maxwell Trophy as the nation's best football player. His No. 60 jersey was retired in 2008.

It was clearly one of the greatest personal matchups in college football in the mid-1960s. Joe Namath had led Alabama to a national championship and an Orange Bowl berth in 1964. Linebacker Tommy Nobis was in the midst of carving a reputation as the greatest defender in Texas football history.

The 1965 Orange Bowl was the first night bowl game in the country, and it was a dream pairing of Bear Bryant's unbeaten No. 1 Crimson Tide and Darrell Royal's 9–1 and fifth-ranked Texas Longhorns. A 14–13 loss to Arkansas was the only blemish on the Texas record. A failed two-point conversion led to that loss and was, arguably, all that had kept the Texas Longhorns from repeating as national champs. Because of that Hog victory, the Razorbacks had won the Southwest Conference and the right to represent the league in the Cotton Bowl Classic, leaving Texas available for the Orange Bowl.

The trip to Miami proved perfect for all concerned: The Orange Bowl matched the national champs of 1963 and 1964 in a nationally televised game that was slotted for New Year's night following the Rose Bowl. Namath, clearly Alabama's most famous player, was matched against the defensive play of Nobis.

Further intrigue entered the picture when Namath reinjured a knee during practice. It appeared for a while that backup Steve Sloan would be the Tide's signal caller. But when Namath was cleared during pregame warm-ups, the battle was on.

Texas used long-distance scoring—a 79-yard touchdown run by Ernie Koy and a 69-yard pass from Jim Hudson to George Sauer—to stun Alabama early, going into halftime with a 21–7 lead. But Namath brought his team back, and late in the game, the Tide had first and goal from the six for a chance to take the lead.

And that brought the collision of the giants of the age. Alabama had moved to the one-yard line by fourth down. Namath took the snap and rammed into right guard. Tom Currie, a Texas defensive tackle, hit him first, but the All-America quarterback slid off and was headed for pay dirt when Nobis met him head on and stopped him just short of the touchdown.

Texas took the ball almost on their own goal line and held on for a 21–17 victory. Alabama fans protested that Namath had, indeed, crossed the plane of the goal, but in the days before instant replay, the winner of the showdown was Nobis, and the winner of the first major bowl game played at night was Texas.

Tailback Ernie Koy (23) takes off on an 80-yard touchdown run as quarterback Marvin Kristynik (12) leads the way against Alabama.

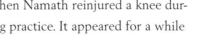

The Mid-1960s Doldrums

For a while, it seemed as though Texas's unparalleled success would go on forever. For five years between 1961 and 1965, Darrell Royal's Longhorns had spent 17 weeks ranked as the No. 1 team in the nation. They had held the top spot for at least two weeks in every one of those years. From the seventh game of the 1960 season through the fourth game of 1965, UT's record was an amazing 48–3–2.

All of that was about to come to a sudden halt in the middle of 1965, however. After all of those wins, Texas lost three straight games. It began in Arkansas, where the No. 1 ranked Longhorns spotted the No. 3 Razorbacks a 20–0 lead, only to fight back and claim a 24–20 margin in the fourth quarter. But Arkansas drove for the winning touchdown in Fayetteville and prevailed by a score of 27–24. With star linebacker Tommy Nobis nursing a knee injury, the downward spiral continued with losses of 20–17 to Rice in Austin and 31–14 at SMU. Although the slide seemed to stop with a win over Baylor the next week, a fourth loss, 25–10 to TCU in Austin, followed the week after that. Once the scourge of the Southwest Conference, Texas finished a pedestrian 6–4 that season. A Bluebonnet Bowl win over Ole Miss stretched the 1966 record to 7–4. The next year, 1967,

Chris Gilbert (25) was the first player in NCAA history to rush for 1,000 yards in each of his seasons of eligibility, 1966–1968. He earned All-America honors and was later inducted into the National Football Foundation's College Hall of Fame.

wasn't much better, with a season-finale loss to Texas A&M capping a 6–4 record. Thus, in the middle of a superlative decade, Texas suddenly went average.

But while there was little to brag about on the varsity level, the excitement around the 40 Acres centered on the five-game seasons of the Texas Yearlings—the freshman teams. At that time, of course, first-year students weren't eligible to compete on the varsity.

The biggest names of the class of 1965 were Chris Gilbert, a stellar running back from Houston, and Bill Bradley, a wondrous athlete from Palestine in East Texas. Bradley, it was said, could kick with both feet and pass with both hands. But as good as those two would become, they paled in reputation to the recruiting class of 1967, which would be officially dubbed The Worster Crowd (pronounced *wooster*). Their namesake, running back Steve Worster, was the most talked-about star of his era. Observers labeled 1967's crop the best Texas recruiting class of all-time. History went a long way toward proving those observers right.

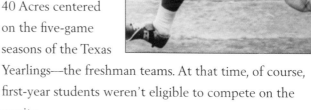

Super Bill Bradley was one of the most heralded athletes ever to come out of a Texas high school when he arrived at the University of Texas as a quarterback in 1965. Bradley played that position for two injury-plagued seasons before he found his niche as a defensive back during the 1968 season.

The Wishbone

Emory Bellard, the Longhorns' backfield coach, sat in his office on a summer day in 1968, smoke curling from his ever-present pipe. A yellow legal pad lay on his desk as an interested coworker stuck his head in his office.

At the time, Texas had been wed to an *I* formation that featured all-conference running back Chris Gilbert at tailback. Bill Bradley had been the option quarterback, and the big question was whether sophomore Steve Worster would beat out junior Ted Koy at wing back.

"So," asked the visitor. "Which one you gonna play?"

Bellard took a puff from his pipe and said in his Texas drawl, "Well, what if we played them both?" He proceeded to draw four circles on his pad, basically in the shape of a *Y*.

"Bradley," he said, pointing to the bottom circle. Then, pointing to the circle above, he said, "Worster." Moving to the upper right of the picture, he said, "Koy." And finally, "Gilbert," as he put a check mark on the circle at the upper left.

Bellard had been working on his idea all summer. He had gone to Darrell Royal that spring and urged that he consider running a version of the Veer offense, which provided a quarterback with various options after a play had already begun. "Give me a formation that has a lead blocker, and I'll consider it," said Royal.

So Bellard tinkered. He convinced staff members to go down into the heat of the non-air-conditioned Gregory Gym to walk through his plan. He called his quarterbacks—Bradley, Joe Norwood, and two youngsters named James Street and Eddie Phillips—to a breakfast meeting in the cafeteria and used salt and pepper shakers, a glass, and a sugar bowl to show them the formation.

Coming off of three seasons in which the Longhorns had lost four games in each, Royal and Bellard were looking for a spark. Bellard's philosophy was based on a series of "reads" by the quarterback. It was a triple-option offense: The first option was to hand off to the fullback; the second and third options involved the quarterback and the trailing halfback. The coaches kept their secret throughout fall practice, finally unveiling it in the first game of the '68 season, a 20–20 tie with the University of Houston.

In a postgame gathering Royal always held with members of the media, sportswriters asked the coach what he was going to call the formation. Several opinions were voiced by the gathered scribes, and finally Mickey Herskowitz of the *Houston Post* compared it to the prime piece of a fried chicken dinner: "It looked like a pulley bone to me."

"Okay," said Royal. "The Wishbone."

It took Bellard and the staff several weeks of trial and error to perfect their creation. The week after the Houston game, Texas Tech beat the Longhorns 31–22, and Street replaced Bradley as the signal caller in the second half. During the next week, the offensive staff prevailed on Bellard to move the fullback back an extra yard from one to two yards behind the quarterback, giving Worster a better chance to read the defense. The Longhorns responded with a 31–3 win over Oklahoma State that Saturday.

Bellard was only in his second year with UT when he devised the Wishbone offense. Before coming to Austin, he'd had a successful career coaching Texas high school football.

Quarterback James Street hands off to fullback Steve Worster in a classic example of the Wishbone offense at work.

But that season's Oklahoma game will always be remembered as the "game that made the Wishbone." The Longhorns and the Sooners were both unranked heading into the game, and Oklahoma led 20–19 when Street brought his offense onto the field at his own 15-yard line with only 2:37 left in the game. Passing from the formation was never the Wishbone's primary characteristic, but some of the biggest plays of the era came from the forward pass. Street completed four passes to put the Longhorns on the Oklahoma 21 with just 55 seconds left. It was then that the Longhorns validated Bellard's concoction. Worster burst for 14 yards on the first play and then rumbled

7 more for the touchdown with only 39 seconds remaining. Texas won 26–20, and the Wishbone was on its way.

By the end of the season, the offense was unstoppable, with Street activating All-America wide receiver Cotton Speyrer and tight end Deryl Comer in the passing game and the triple option threat in the running game. Gilbert became the first back in NCAA history to rush for at least 1,000 yards in each of the seasons for which he was eligible. He earned All-America honors and was later inducted into the National Football Foundation's College Hall of Fame.

Texas finished the regular season ranked 5th in the nation and beat No. 8 Tennessee 36–13 in the Cotton Bowl Classic.

This plaque would have looked perfect on any Longhorns fan's wall in the early 1960s.

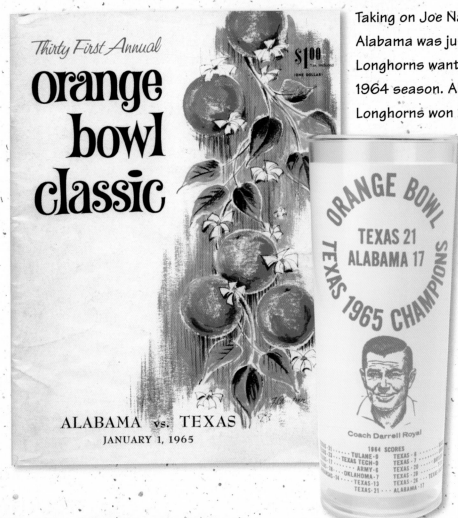

Thirty First Annual

orange bowl classic

$1.00
Tax Included
(ONE DOLLAR)

ALABAMA vs. TEXAS
JANUARY 1, 1965

ORANGE BOWL
TEXAS 21
ALABAMA 17
TEXAS 1965 CHAMPIONS

Coach Darrell Royal

1964 SCORES

Taking on Joe Namath and No. 1 Alabama was just what the Longhorns wanted to cap their 1964 season. Although the No. 5 Longhorns won 21–17, it didn't help their final ranking, which remained at No. 5.

Ideal for waving at the game or pinning up on the wall, this Longhorn pennant declares its owner's colors.

OKLA VS TEXAS
THE SOUTHWEST CLASSIC
63RD ANNUAL GAME

COTTON BOWL · DALLAS · OCT. 12, 1968

SOUVENIR PROGRAM 50¢

Longhorns Fleece Vols in Cotton Bowl
January 1, 1969
Texas Takes Down Tennessee 36–13

It was bound to be a victory for orange as the Texas Longhorns faced down the Tennessee Volunteers in the 43rd Cotton Bowl Classic, but it was the Texas shade of burnt orange that won the day. James Street led his team to an all-out assault on the Vols, attacking on the ground and in the air. Two long-distance receptions of 78 yards and 79 yards by Charles "Cotton" Speyrer added dazzle to the day's performance. The Longhorns' Wishbone offense is now a full-blown spectacle as opposing defenses search for a way to shut it down.

The 1968 game against Oklahoma is where the Wishbone offense proved itself. James Street and Steve Worster used it to clinch the game with only 39 seconds left on the clock.

Were the Longhorns No. 1? A light tap on the top of this bobblehead's helmet set it to nodding yes.

After Robert Heard selected some of Darrell Royal's most colorful comments and sayings for this book, they came to be called "Royalisms."

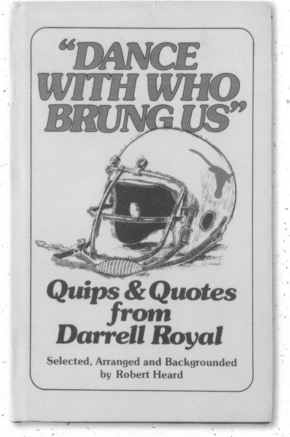

"DANCE WITH WHO BRUNG US"

Quips & Quotes from Darrell Royal

Selected, Arranged and Backgrounded by Robert Heard

Integration

Julius Whittier and Roosevelt Leaks brought power to the Longhorns in the early 1970s. Their success paved the way for more African Americans to choose to play for Texas.

The winds of change had come slowly to the Southwest Conference. Supreme Court decisions in the 1950s had mandated that schools in the United States be integrated. The University of Texas had been in the spotlight of this evolution when a young African American man named Hemann Sweatt won a suit to enter Texas Law School in 1950.

But while the university was integrated, the athletics programs were not. That began to change in 1964, about the same time President Lyndon B. Johnson was pushing through an extensive civil rights bill. That spring, segregation was officially ended in SWC athletics programs, and UT was the first to break the "color" line when two African Americans participated in track that year.

In football, SMU and Baylor recruited the first African American athletes in the fall of 1965, and three seasons

later, the University of Texas welcomed its first scholarship freshman player in Leon O'Neal. O'Neal left after his freshman season in 1968, and a couple of walk-ons, E. A. Curry and Robinson Parsons, also participated with the varsity that year.

The first African American to receive a varsity letter was Julius Whittier, a San Antonio native who played offensive line and tight end during his three years on the varsity from 1970 through 1972. But while Whittier was the first letter winner, the player who changed the face of Texas football was Roosevelt Leaks, the team's first African American star.

Leaks, from Brenham, Texas, was the perfect choice for fullback in the Wishbone formation when he made the varsity as a sophomore in 1972. With power and speed, the soft-spoken Leaks rushed for more than 1,000 yards in both of his first two seasons—an even more significant statistic given that he played in a era when teams had only ten regular season games and bowl games did not count in NCAA statistics. He earned All-America honors and finished third in the Heisman Trophy voting in 1973, a year in which he also set a single-game school rushing record with 342 yards against SMU.

A knee injured during practice in 1974 severely limited Leaks's senior season, but his presence at Texas had cleared the way for Darrell Royal's Longhorn staff to attract more African American players. And because of Roosevelt Leaks, a young running back in Tyler, Texas, discounted negative recruiting and chose to come to Texas. After he arrived on the UT campus, nothing would ever be the same. His name was Earl Campbell.

The Loyal Lieutenants

Two years separated their arrival on the Texas campus, but for most of Darrell Royal's 20 seasons, Mike Campbell and Bill Ellington were his most trusted aides.

Campbell had been a high school coach in Mississippi, and he joined Royal's staff at Mississippi State, becoming the driving force behind every defense Royal's teams put on the field during his tenure. A fixture at Longhorn football practices was a tall tower from where Royal could view the workouts, always checking the offense to his left and the defense to his right. When Royal came down from that tower, players and coaches alike hoped he'd go to the other side of the field—to a person, they knew he had seen something he wanted to correct. Most of the time, Royal would head left, leaving Campbell in complete control of the defense.

Ellington was one of the most popular men in the Texas Athletics Department. He joined the staff as a football coach in 1959, and in 1968 he assumed duties as the only assistant athletics director that Royal ever had. Ellington had been a highly successful high school coach in Texas, leading Garland to the state Class AAA championship, among many accomplishments at the prep school level.

In the years before freshmen were eligible to play for the varsity team, Ellington brought the UT rookies their first experience of college football as the head freshman team coach. Over the five-game seasons in which they competed, the Texas Yearlings under his leadership earned the most successful record in the Southwest Conference. In a time when teams were allowed to scout opponents in person, Ellington always drew the task of viewing the rival Oklahoma Sooners first-hand. During his tenure in that role, Texas lost only once in 11 games.

Ellington eventually gave up his on-the-field coaching duties to work full-time as an administrator. When Royal chose to retire as athletics director in the fall of 1979, Ellington served a year and a half in that position.

Mike Campbell's career followed a different path. When Royal stepped down from coaching in 1976, he tabbed Campbell as the person he wanted to replace him as the head football coach. But in a power struggle with the highest level of UT administrators, Royal's wishes were ignored. Campbell, who had turned down several head coaching opportunities during his time at Texas, stepped away from the game. He ultimately returned to the UT Athletics Department as head of the Texas Longhorn Education Foundation and, until he died in 1998, was still regarded as one of the most knowledgeable football minds in the country.

Bill Ellington was a high school coach when Darrell Royal hired him in 1959.

Assistant coach Mike Campbell was Royal's chief lieutenant. Campbell, whose three sons would play for the team, was the architect of some of the greatest Longhorn defenses. He was inducted into the Longhorn Hall of Honor in 1984, the only Texas assistant ever accorded such an honor.

Frank Erwin and the Tree Huggers

Frank C. Erwin, Jr., was one of the most powerful men in University of Texas history. He was very politically connected—on a first-name basis with the president of the United States, the governor of Texas, and every other important politician in between. Erwin's vocation was as an attorney. But his avocation was UT, and specifically UT athletics.

The University of Texas is a component institution of the University of Texas System, and that network is run by a board of regents—nine people who oversee all the operations of a vast economic and educational empire. Erwin was a regent, and by 1969 he was serving as chairman of the board. In fact, until the day he died in 1980, he was addressed as "Mr. Chairman."

The 1960s were a time of football and flower children on the Texas campus, and most of the time the two coex-isted remarkably well. But the expansion of Texas Memorial Stadium became a cause for conflict between them. As part of the renovation, San Jacinto Boulevard, which ran just to the west, had to be moved toward Waller Creek, which in turn required the removal of some impressive trees. The hippies rose up defiantly. In fact, when it came time for the bulldozers to remove the trees, the protesters rose all the way up into them.

Erwin was at the site that day, anticipating a fight. It was under his orders that the only blow in the battle was delivered. Even though students were clinging to the branches, Erwin directed the bulldozers to get the job started and begin pushing down the trees. Because the rebellious students had removed ribbons from the few trees that had been designated for removal, more trees were knocked down than had been originally intended.

Erwin barely blinked when the media came to interview him on the matter, calling the tree-lovers "a bunch of dirty nuthin's." With that, San Jacinto Boulevard was redirected to its new location, and the stadium construction was under way.

Due to confusion caused by the conflict, more trees were lost along Waller Creek than called for in the initial plan.

Some of the protesters had to be physically removed from the trees before the bulldozers could move in to take them down.

James Street Rises to the Occasion

The new quarterback received what Mike Campbell, Darrell Royal's trusted assistant, commonly referred to as a "battlefield promotion"—when a reserve player becomes a starter in the midst of a game. Texas was facing Texas Tech in 1968—the second game of the Wishbone offense—and things had not gone well for the starter, the celebrated Bill Bradley. Frustrated, Darrell Royal grabbed Bradley's back-up by the arm and thrust him into the game. And so it was that James Street, a junior from Longview, Texas, who had come to UT as both a baseball and football player, began a football career that would create a legend.

Street had established himself on the baseball field the previous spring, hurling the Longhorns to the Southwest Conference championship and earning a trip to the NCAA College World Series for new coach Cliff Gustafson. Now, he assumed the task of leading the Longhorn football team out of a funk that had included three consecutive four-loss seasons. And that's just what Street did. While the Longhorns fell short in Street's comeback attempt in Lubbock, the 31–22 loss was the last defeat they would suffer for 30 games, and Street would be personally responsible for quarterbacking them to 20 straight wins before finishing his eligibility.

His UT baseball career was not at an end, however. While he was going unbeaten as starting quarterback, he was also receiving high marks as a right-handed pitcher with a wicked curve ball. He earned All-Southwest Conference honors on the mound for three consecutive years, each season helping lead the Longhorns to the CWS. Street was also picked as the All-Southwest Conference

quarterback in 1969, making him one of the few Longhorns in the post–World War II era to be chosen all-league in two sports.

More than 30 years later, Street's fame would be revisited in both sports but for different reasons. The Longhorns' 2005 national championship run produced the first UT unbeaten season since 1969. But Street's legacy would be felt more personally in baseball.

In 2002, James Street's son Huston became an All-America relief pitcher as a freshman at UT, earning MVP honors as Texas won the NCAA College World Series. Following two more successful seasons at Texas, Huston was named American League Rookie of the Year as a closer for the Oakland Athletics.

And what were Royal's words of wisdom on that night when he thrust Street into the game against Texas Tech and began this magnificent career? "He looked me straight in the eye," remembered Street, "and said, 'Hell, you can't do any worse!'"

If you can't go through, go over. James Street had a knack for getting past the opposition.

The Game of the Century

Momentum shifted to Texas in the fourth quarter. Jim Bertelsen just gets over the goal line for the second Longhorn touchdown to tie the game. An extra point was all UT needed for the margin of victory.

It had been the brainchild of television executive Beano Cook, who had been looking for a way that his network, ABC, could provide an appropriate conclusion to the 100th year of college football. At the time, the NCAA controlled the televising of all college football, and their sole carrier for live regular-season games was ABC Sports. Veteran announcer Chris Schenkel did the play by play, with color commentary from the venerable Bud Wilkinson, who stepped into the TV booth after ending his college coaching career at the University of Oklahoma.

Throughout the 1969 season, the NCAA had observed the centennial celebration of the day that Rutgers and Princeton gathered on a primitive field to play the first college football game. Tributes were held, and teams—including Texas—wore football-shape patches with the number "100" in their respective school colors.

Before the schedule had been set for that season, Cook had come up with the idea of moving a regular-season rivalry game to December 6, a week after the regular season had concluded. Looking at the schedules of the various

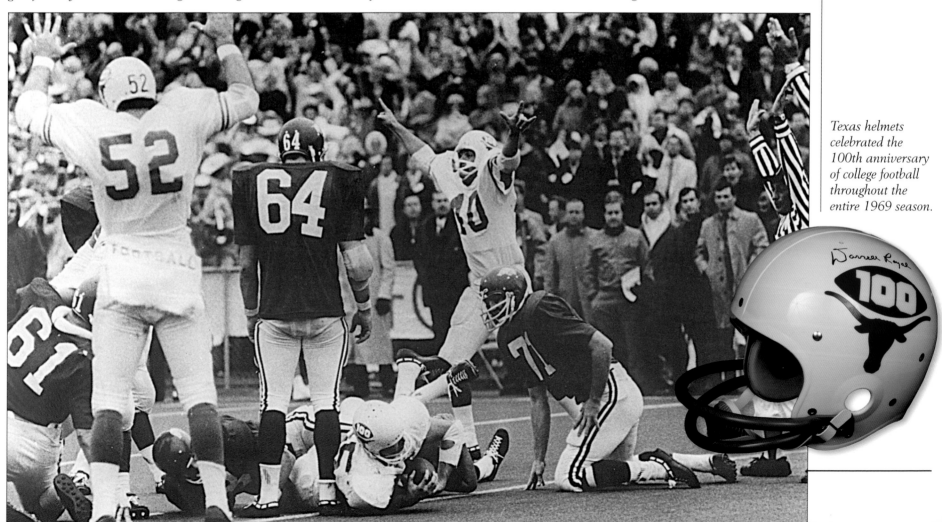

Texas helmets celebrated the 100th anniversary of college football throughout the entire 1969 season.

teams, Beano determined that Texas and Arkansas had the best chance to end the regular season unbeaten—as long, of course, as they didn't play each other. The two programs had been excellent for most of the decade. Frank Broyles's Arkansas Razorbacks had finished the 1964 season unbeaten and had maintained a high level of play. Despite a slump in the mid-'60s, Royal's Longhorns were in the process of earning the title "Team of the Decade"—ABC itself would later name Royal "Coach of the Decade." So the two schools agreed to move their game from the third week in October to the end of the year.

Texas was in the second year of its Wishbone offense and was crushing opponents. Arkansas had a good defense, a wide-open passing game, and a great kicker. As the season progressed, both teams just kept winning.

In his wildest dreams, Cook could never have imagined the ultimate result of his plan. Both teams were ranked in the Top 10, but until the weekend before Thanksgiving, everybody in the country thought that Ohio State, national champs in 1968, were on their way to a second straight title. But as Texas enjoyed a week off before their upcoming Thanksgiving Day game with Texas A&M in College Station, a rookie coach named Bo Schembechler guided Michigan to a stunning upset of the Buckeyes. When the smoke cleared, Texas was No. 1, Arkansas No. 2, and unbeaten Penn State was lobbying to get into the national championship race. But the Nittany Lions would be frustrated, not only by the polls, but by the president of the United States himself. Richard M. Nixon, at the urging of the NCAA and ABC, agreed to attend the Texas-Arkansas game in Fayetteville and present a plaque to the winner—proclaiming them champions of the 100th season of college football.

As the game approached, it rapidly became a "happening." Evangelist Billy Graham came to give the pregame prayer. Country singer and TV personality Roy Clark was there for the national anthem. And as President Nixon's helicopter landed on a field south of the stadium just before kickoff, his official party included the congressman from Houston, George H. W. Bush.

During the many years that Royal and Broyles competed against each other, one phenomenon emerged: Arkansas always entered the fray "hoping" to win, while Texas came "expecting" to win. At this point of their rivalry, Royal's teams had won 7 of the 11 meetings between the two. While the entire state of Arkansas rallied around Fayetteville on that first weekend of December, Texas was getting a send-off back in Austin at a pep rally attended by nearly 30,000 fans.

The night before the game, a cold rain began to fall. By game time, it was alternately spitting rain and snow. For much of the game, it seemed Arkansas would prevail—at the end of three quarters, Texas trailed 14–0. That, however, became an opportunity for Royal, quarterback James Street, and the Longhorns to secure immortality as far as Texas football was concerned. In front of one of the largest television audiences up to that time—literally half the TV sets in use in the country were watching the game—the Longhorns scored 15 fourth-quarter points to win and to claim President Nixon's plaque.

Presidential politics were put aside in celebration of the 100th year of college football. President Richard Nixon presented a plaque to Darrell Royal, captains Ted Koy (24) and James Street (16), and the victorious Longhorns.

The Littlest Longhorn

When he first came to Texas, Freddie Steinmark was known as "the littlest Longhorn." When he died of a rare form of bone cancer just four years later, he would forever be remembered as the Longhorn with the biggest heart.

Fred Steinmark and his best friend, Bobby Mitchell, were rarities when they arrived in Austin from the Denver suburb of Wheat Ridge, Colorado. Darrell Royal and his staff seldom recruited out of state, but Steinmark's remarkable quickness and Mitchell's savvy on the offensive line made them hard to ignore. As a sophomore in 1968, Steinmark led the team in punt returns and established himself at safety as the anchor of a three-deep secondary. By his junior season of 1969, he had become a defensive leader.

But as the campaign to the national championship of 1969 progressed, Steinmark appeared troubled by a nagging injury that doctors had originally thought was a bruise. In the final game of the season, with the Longhorns trailing Arkansas 14–8, Steinmark had been beaten on a Razorback pass play. Chuck Dicus, the Arkansas receiver, appeared destined for a touchdown, until Freddie reached out and grabbed him at the Texas ten-yard line, resulting in a pass interference penalty.

The Longhorns eventually stopped the drive with an interception, but Steinmark, who could no longer run, had yielded the field to his backup Rick Nabors by the time Texas clinched the 15–14 victory. On returning to Austin, Freddie went to see the team physician, who X-rayed his leg and discovered a spot on the bone. The safety was rushed to M. D. Anderson Cancer Center in Houston. Six days after Freddie Steinmark had played for the national championship, doctors amputated his left leg. The spot on the bone had turned out to be an osteogenic sarcoma—a deadly type of bone cancer.

A Catholic, Freddie had grown up dreaming of playing for Notre Dame, the Longhorns' scheduled opponents in the upcoming Cotton Bowl. Steinmark had his surgery on December 12 and vowed to attend the New Year's Day game in Dallas. One of the more emotional moments in Cotton Bowl history saw Steinmark, dressed in a long jacket and with his pants neatly folded where his leg had been, come down the ramp of the tunnel on his crutches. Supported by those crutches, he stood on the sidelines for the entire game. Coach Royal gave him the game ball in the locker room after the Longhorns' 21–17 victory.

Steinmark lived for a year and a half following the surgery, serving as a graduate assistant on the coaching staff. On completion of the remodeled Texas Memorial Stadium in 1972, the south-end scoreboard was dedicated as the "Freddie Steinmark Scoreboard." When Coach Mack Brown came to Texas in 1998, he put Steinmark's picture on the scoreboard. Now Longhorn players entering and leaving the field touch that picture to honor Steinmark's courage.

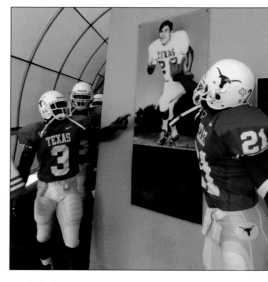

Steinmark's picture is at the back of the scoreboard that bears his name, serving as inspiration to the Longhorns.

Only 19 days after his left leg was amputated, Freddie Steinmark attended the 1970 Cotton Bowl, standing on the sidelines throughout the game, to watch his teammates defeat Notre Dame 21–17.

The Irish Are Coming

With the 1969 national championship decided in the Longhorns' favor, there was still one more drama left to play out in the centennial year of college football: the Cotton Bowl Classic on January 1, 1970.

Notre Dame, a name synonymous with college football, had removed itself from post-season bowl competition after the 1925 Rose Bowl, when the famous Four Horsemen led the Irish to a 27–10 win over Stanford. But now, 45 years later, Cotton Bowl emissaries Field Scovell and Wilbur Evans had coaxed the Irish, the ninth-ranked team in the country, into playing in their game. After the December 6 Arkansas showdown, the glamour of the Irish further extended the Longhorns' profile in what was arguably their most dramatic season finish ever.

Ara Parseghian's muscular Notre Dame team sported an 8–1–1 record, losing only to troublesome Purdue and tying Southern California. And they were led by quarterback Joe Theismann. Heavy rains the week of the Cotton Bowl game had turned the stadium's turf into a chopped-up mess. Despite the use of helicopters from a nearby air base in an effort to dry the field, conditions remained sloppy.

Theismann, already heralded as a Heisman Trophy candidate, hurled his team to two leads, first at 10–0 and later at 17–14. But Texas had its superstar at quarterback, the charismatic James Street. Street, starting his 20th consecutive game for the Longhorns, had never lost as UT's No. 1 signal caller. And he didn't intend to lose this one.

Theismann's touchdown pass with 6:52 left in the game put the Irish up by three, and Texas was 76 yards away from the goal line when Street walked onto the field for his final drive as a Longhorn. Street pushed forward to the Irish 20-yard line where, in a fourth-and-two situation, halfback Ted Koy rushed for two yards and a foot. But four downs and eight yards later, with 2:26 remaining in the game, Texas faced another fourth and two. Royal and Street conferred, and a picture taken by photographer Linda Kaye captured the moment: The scoreboard behind them read, "14 Texas, 2:26 remaining, Notre Dame 17, 4 down 2 to go, ball on 10, Quarter 4." Street returned to the field, completed an eight-yard pass to diving wide receiver Cotton Speyrer, and the Longhorns soon scored the winning touchdown. A final interception stopped Theismann's last drive.

Royal, who had been credited for disdaining the forward pass, had now won two games with late aerial plays. That prompted the elderly gentleman who ran the elevator in the Cotton Bowl press box to comment after the game, "I sure wouldn't want to get in a card game with that Darrell Royal. Man, is he a riverboat gambler."

Linda Kaye's famous photo conveys all the drama of the situation: Street and Royal confer on what may be their last chance—if they are wrong, it could mean losing the game. But they're not wrong.

TEXAS MEMORIES

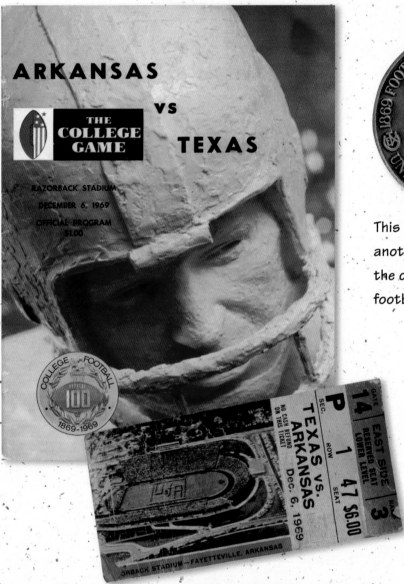

This medallion was another recognition of the centennial of college football.

You couldn't have asked for a better matchup for the "Game of the Century"—No. 1 Texas against No. 2 Arkansas in the last game of the season. The Longhorns scored all their points in the fourth quarter, leading to a 15–14 UT win. President Richard Nixon personally presented the winning team with a championship plaque.

The 1960s in Texas football were celebrated in this record album, which featured interviews with players past and present as well as musical numbers by the Longhorn band.

The Texas Longhorn on this sticker is ready to take on all comers who might challenge UT's No. 1 status on college football's 100th anniversary.

The very first Longhorn game of the 1970s had more than its share of excitement. The 21–17 victory over Notre Dame had the distinction of being Texas's 500th win.

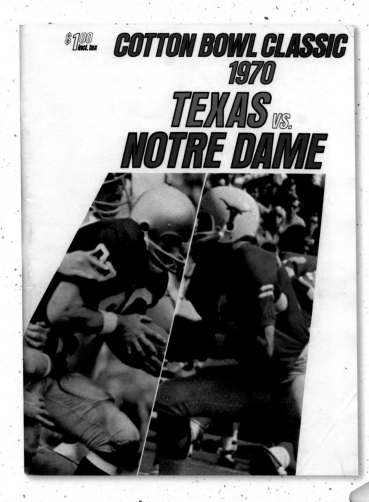

COTTON BOWL CLASSIC 1970
$1.00 incl. tax
TEXAS vs. NOTRE DAME

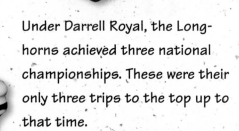

NATIONAL COLLEGIATE
Champions
THE UNIVERSITY OF TEXAS
1963, 1969, 1970

FOOTBALL

Under Darrell Royal, the Longhorns achieved three national championships. These were their only three trips to the top up to that time.

WOOSTER BOOSTERS
Courtesy: BERT'S BAR-B-Q – 610 West 19th Street
FOR HEISMANN TROPHY 1970

More concerned with rhyming than spelling, this bumper sticker supported Steve Worster's quest for a Heisman Trophy. He finished fourth in the voting for 1970.

Hook 'em HORNS!
TEXAS 1 TEXA-1
COMMEMORATIVE
30 STRAIGHT VICTORIES

From October 5, 1968, until December 5, 1970—the better part of three seasons—the Longhorns never lost a game. In two of those seasons, Texas brought home national championships.

A Second Year at the Top

In the more than 50 years between the 1957 and the 2008 seasons, only two teams repeated as national champions in the year-end Coaches Poll, which was first conducted by United Press International and later by ESPN/*USA Today*. And until Nebraska pulled it off in the mid-1990s, only Texas had won back-to-back titles—in 1969 and 1970.

The Worster Crowd was in its senior season in 1970, and once junior Eddie Phillips took over quarterbacking chores from the departed James Street, Texas settled in for one of the greatest runs of the era. That winning streak, which had begun with the third game of 1968, stretched to 20 games by the beginning of the season. With fullback Steve Worster, halfback Jim Bertelsen, and wide receiver Cotton Speyrer returning to an offense powered up front by All-America tackle Bobby Wuensch, Phillips was the only question mark on the offensive side of the ball. Defensively, end Bill Atessis and linebacker Scott Henderson returned, along with a solid corps from the 1969 national champs.

The Wishbone was rolling as Phillips led the No. 2 ranked Longhorns to a reassuring 56–15 victory over California in the season opener. An easy victory over Texas Tech followed, but as Texas sought its 23rd-straight victory in a game against UCLA in Austin, something went dreadfully wrong.

Tommy Prothro, the head coach at UCLA, had analyzed the Wishbone and come up with a defense that would stop the Longhorns. On the first series, Phillips pitched the ball on a blind toss back to his running back, Billy Dale. It had always worked before, but this time the ball hit a crashing Bruin defender in the back of the helmet. The result was shocking and devastating, and the Longhorns struggled to adjust. The UCLA defense caused them so many problems that the Longhorns appeared to be on the ropes as the game neared its conclusion. Trailing 17–13 with 20 seconds remaining, the Longhorns were at the UCLA 45.

Darrell Royal and tri-captains James Street, Ted Koy, and Glenn Halsell with the MacArthur Bowl in 1969.

Dominating the '60s

At the end of the 1970 season, ABC-TV—the only network carrying NCAA regular-season college football games—named Darrell Royal "Coach of the Decade." It wasn't hard to figure out why.

In the years from 1961 through 1970, Royal's teams won six Southwest Conference championships and three national championships; finished in the Top 5 seven times; and went to eight bowl games, winning six of them.

The records:

1961: 10–1, SWC Champs, No. 3 national ranking

1962: 9–1–1, SWC Champs, No. 4 national ranking

1963: 11–0, SWC Champs, national champions

1964: 10–1, No. 5 national ranking

1968: 9–1–1, SWC Champs, No. 3 national ranking

1969: 11–0, SWC Champs, national champions

1970: 10–1, SWC Champs, UPI national champions, No. 3 AP

In his 20-year career, Royal would coach teams to 11 Southwest Conference championships and 16 bowl games. Nine of his teams finished the year ranked among the nation's Top 5.

Sports Illustrated
DECEMBER 14, 1970 60 CENTS
TEXAS SLAUGHTERS ARKANSAS

Woo Woo Worster on a Rampage

Steve Worster became the public face of the Longhorns in this issue of Sports Illustrated *published at the end of the season.*

Phillips dropped back to pass and spotted tight end Tommy Woodard and Speyrer, his All-America receiver, near each other at the Bruin 25. As the ball sailed over Woodard, Speyrer made a leaping catch. The two UCLA defensive backs, drawn together by the receivers' routes, collided. Speyrer landed and, in the same motion, spun toward the goal line, past the final UCLA defender. With 12 seconds remaining, he made the winning touchdown. Observers in the temporary press box looked out over a student section that glistened in a shower of cups, ice, and anything else the students could toss in the air.

After the game, the Texas coaches adjusted their offense, providing a lead blocker on the option pitch, and the Wishbone was rolling again. Texas crushed Oklahoma 41–9 and then rolled on to a second "Big Shootout" with Arkansas at the end of the season. The philosophy of ABC-TV seemed to be that if it worked once, it should work again, and Arkansas coach Frank Broyles agreed. By the time of the December 5 game in Austin, Texas was No. 1 and the Razorbacks were No. 4.

Broyles was content with what his defense had done against the Longhorns in 1969, and he changed little in his plan of attack. In addition to tweaking their offense after UCLA, however, Darrell Royal and his staff had inserted some other surprises. As a result, Texas blew the Razorbacks away 42–7.

The Longhorns again claimed the UPI National Championship and shared the National Football Foundation's MacArthur Bowl Trophy with Ohio State. The Associated Press trophy that season, however, wasn't presented until after the season's bowl games.

Ranked No. 1 and riding a 30-game winning streak, the Longhorns' finally lost 24–11 in a Cotton Bowl rematch against No. 6–rated Notre Dame on January 1, 1971. But as the new decade was getting under way, Royal had made the Texas football program one of the best in all of collegiate athletics. The budget was $705,250, and the self-sustaining athletic budget (with almost all of the income coming from football) was $1,628,000. And with 15,000 new seats coming in Texas Memorial Stadium, the money was rolling in.

Darrell Royal confers with quarterback Eddie Phillips on the sidelines of the televised end-of-the-year rematch with Arkansas. The No. 1 Longhorns roll over the No. 4 Razorbacks 42–7.

A Growing Stadium for a Growing Team

The 1968 Texas-Houston game was the final straw. Texas Memorial Stadium, built in 1924, had been expanded and improved with lights and other paraphernalia, but as the 1960s came to a close, this aging showcase for college football had been outgrown. When 66,000 folks showed up for the season opener against Houston in 1968, half of the stadium had been virtually given away to students from the two institutions. Economics dictated a change, and the two most powerful men at the University of Texas—football coach Darrell Royal and Regent Frank C. Erwin, Jr.—were on the same page for a change.

Texas was faced with two options: Add seats to the stadium or head away from campus to land owned by the university in northwest Austin and build a new stadium. Royal lobbied for the on-campus plan because he believed it would continue a bond with the student body and the greater university. It was one of the few times in their tenure as power brokers for UT athletics that Royal and Erwin agreed. So plans were made for the addition of a 15,000-seat deck on the west side.

The initial part of the "new look" actually came in 1969, when UT became one of the first universities in the country to install Astroturf, a synthetic outdoor field surface that had been invented for the Houston Astrodome. Following the 1969 season, the old press box was taken down, and construction began on the new deck. Royal—with help from Athletics Council chairman Neils Thompson (a civil engineering professor)—came up with an innovative plan for an 11-story building underneath the deck. The new upper deck would essentially act as the roof on a facility that would hold gymnasiums, classrooms, and offices. The cost was somewhere around $20 million.

As the 1970 season approached, construction of the building and deck had reached only the top of the west stands and the lights had been removed. So Texas played its home games that season at 4 P.M. with a wooden-frame press box on top of the east stands.

Much of the superstructure was completed by the 1971 season, so UT had partial use of the new seats. Construction was entirely completed by the opening game of 1972, raising the official capacity of the stadium to 77,809.

Texas Memorial Stadium underwent a facelift in the early 1970s. Instead of moving elsewhere to build a brand-new venue, the university decided to add 15,000 seats to accommodate growing crowds.

Royalisms

Darrell Royal was as famous for his wit and wisdom as he was for his football victories. Here are some of his most famous quotes:

"We're gonna dance with who brung us."

"Ole ugly is better than ole nuthin'."

"He's so rich he could burn a wet elephant."

"They're hotter than a burning stump."

"We live one day at a time and scratch where it itches."

"You're what-iffing now, and everybody can what-if."

"Punt returns will kill you before a minnow can swim a dipper."

"Every coach likes those players who, like trained pigs, will grin and jump right into the slop."

"They didn't exactly come into town on a load of wood."

"When that adrenaline starts flowing, you just get there faster than normal. You can jump higher and dive deeper and come up drier."

"Winning coaches must treat mistakes like copperheads in the bedclothes—avoid them with all the energy you can muster."

"Breaks balance out. The sun don't shine on the same ole dog's rear end every day."

"A little bit of perfume won't hurt if you don't drink it."

"To say we were the only ones aggressive would be like a skunk telling a possum that his breath smells."

"Luck is what happens when preparation meets opportunity."

After losing a close game in the final minutes after his team had taken the lead: "It was like having a big ole lollipop in your mouth, and the first thing you know all you have left is the stick."

Talking to his team at halftime of a game in which they were trailing: "There's a heckuva a fight going on out there. Why don't you get in on it?"

"Next to bad weather, there is no equalizer like two fired-up football teams."

"You can't invent a feeling."

"We're not exactly a rolling ball of butcher knives."

Royal was always quick with a folksy turn of phrase or clever Texas saying. Some of his Royalisms have even been picked up and widely used by others.

On recruiting: "Give me the guy with his jaw stuck out, his shirt sleeves rolled up, and who swaggers when he walks. I know it's Harry High School, but if I have to make a choice, I'll take the cocky, overconfident, conceited kid over the one who has so much humility he can't look you in the eye."

"You've got to adjust. Changes are necessary with all kinds of science and technology, so why should it be any different with people? I don't think the kid's preference for long hair and mustaches is all that important. Football is still a good game, but we do need to make some changes. The tail should never wag the dog, but as long as football is in its proper place on the campus, then it's good. I want to be remembered as a winning coach, but I also want to be remembered as an honest and ethical coach."

Royal's Last Lap

By 1971, Darrell Royal was only 47 years old, and he had done everything there was to do in college football. In the previous eight years, his team had won three national championships. He had been named national coach of the year several times, and his team had won three straight Southwest Conference titles and had just finished a 30-game winning streak.

With his Wishbone offense, he had changed the landscape of college football. His friend Paul "Bear" Bryant at

Royal confers with quarterback Marty Akins on the sidelines during a 1973 game.

Alabama and his arch-rival Oklahoma were both either looking at the possibilities of adopting the offense or had already done so.

But college football recruiting was beginning to change. In perhaps the most significant development of the era, as of the 1972 season, first-year students officially became eligible to play on the varsity team. Equally important in the Southwest, however, was the developing arms race in recruiting African American athletes. To the north, Oklahoma had broken ahead in the battle for black athletes in the late 1950s with the appearance of Prentice Gautt, an outstanding running back.

The great Texas recruiting class of 1967 had departed, but quarterback Eddie Phillips had emerged as perhaps the best Wishbone quarterback in history. So when Texas traveled to Los Angeles to open the season at the Coliseum against UCLA, the Longhorns carried a No. 3 national ranking. The game ended in a 28–10 victory, but as Phillips was wrapping it up, he pulled a hamstring in his right leg—an injury that would haunt the Longhorns throughout the season.

Texas went on to win the Southwest Conference, though the Longhorns experienced a loss to Oklahoma 48–27 in only the second Sooner victory over Texas in 14 years. Texas then fell to Arkansas 31–7 as quarterbacks Phillips and Donnie Wigginton were both injured. In the Cotton Bowl Classic, Penn State finally got its revenge for the disputed end of the 1969 season, defeating UT 30–6.

Although Texas prospects seemed to be headed downhill, the 1972 season found the university right back in the mix for national honors. A win over Alabama in the

Cotton Bowl game capped a 10–1 season, and the Longhorns once again finished in the Top 10 nationally. Roosevelt Leaks emerged as a legitimate star at fullback, and Alan Lowry completed a rare feat: earning All–Southwest Conference honors at quarterback after being named an all-conference defensive back the year before. The season also featured offensive tackle Jerry Sisemore, one of the greatest linemen in UT history.

In 1973, Texas extended its record string of Southwest Conference championships, earning its sixth straight in an 8–3 campaign. The Longhorns had begun the season with a No. 1 prediction from *Sports Illustrated*, but an opening loss to Miami dropped them from the national rankings for the first time since early in the 1968 season.

For the next three seasons, Marty Akins emerged as the master signal caller of the Wishbone. Leaks earned All-America honors during the 1973 campaign—a feat that eventually propelled him to the National Football Foundation's College Hall of Fame. But the biggest victory of the 1973 season didn't come on the field. It was, rather, the recruiting battle that earned the Longhorns a young running back named Earl Campbell. In 1974, Campbell was thrust into the starting fullback role after Leaks suffered a knee injury.

In 1974, college football added an 11th game to the regular season, and the Longhorns finished 8–3. Losses at Texas Tech and Baylor cost them a seventh straight SWC title. Ranked No. 11 heading into a Gator Bowl meeting with No. 6 Auburn, Texas fell 27–3.

By 1975, Texas A&M was beginning to emerge from a long slumber. Despite a stellar season from Campbell, the Longhorns were forced to share a three-way tie for the Southwest Conference title. When the Aggies beat Texas, suffering from an injury to Akins, 20–10, both Arkansas

and Texas A&M were on top alongside the Longhorns. Texas bounced back with a come-from-behind, 38–21 victory over Colorado in the Bluebonnet Bowl. The game featured Campbell as a running back in the Wishbone…a harbinger of things to come.

Following the final fall scrimmage of the 1976 season, a concerned Darrell Royal met with the media and, in response to a question about Texas prospects, said, "It looked like a 5–5 team to me." The talent that year was young, and much of it experienced injury. Earl Campbell, who came in weighing a hefty 242 pounds, suffered a hamstring pull that forced him to miss most or all of five games. Safety Johnnie Johnson, who earned induction in the NFF College Hall of Fame years later, missed most of the year with a bruised muscle. Even the highlights were bittersweet. A 6–6 tie with No. 3 Oklahoma stopped a five-game Sooner winning streak. And finally, Texas and Arkansas once more moved their game from October to the end of the season for ABC television.

When the decision was made to move the game, no one could have anticipated that it would have extraordinary significance. As the final game of 1976 ended, longtime friends and foes Darrell Royal and Frank Broyles of Arkansas retired as coaches at their respective institutions. Royal, who went on to serve as athletics director for three years, was 52 years old.

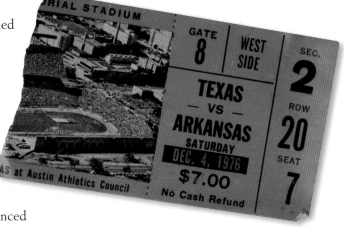

The year-end game against Arkansas in 1976 was Darrell Royal's last as head coach. His final season saw a 5–5–1 record, but he went out on a high note, defeating the Razorbacks 29–12.

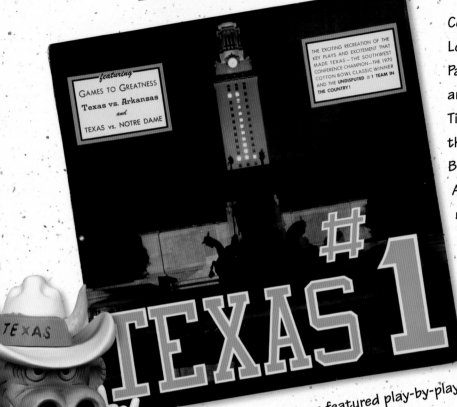

TEXAS #1

featuring
GAMES TO GREATNESS
Texas vs. Arkansas
and
TEXAS vs. NOTRE DAME

THE EXCITING RECREATION OF THE KEY PLAYS AND EXCITEMENT THAT MADE TEXAS — THE SOUTHWEST CONFERENCE CHAMPION—THE 1970 COTTON BOWL CLASSIC WINNER AND THE UNDISPUTED # 1 TEAM IN THE COUNTRY!

Although this record album featured play-by-play re-creations of vital moments and games from Texas's 1969 national championship season, its back cover promised "the actual voices of Darrell Royal and Richard Nixon."

No Texas football gathering was complete without this Longhorn decanter. Who wouldn't want to refill a glass from the steer's nostrils?

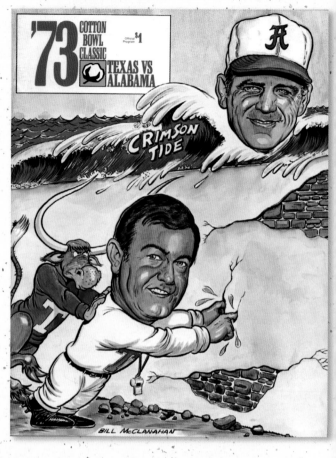

'73 COTTON BOWL CLASSIC
Official $1
TEXAS VS ALABAMA

CRIMSON TIDE

BILL McCLANAHAN

Could Royal and his Longhorns hold back Paul "Bear" Bryant and the Crimson Tide of Alabama in the 1973 Cotton Bowl? Although Alabama was ranked higher than Texas, the answer was yes, as UT triumphed 17–13.

LONGHORNS FOR McGOVERN

LONGHORNS FOR NIXON

Politics came onto the UT campus during the 1972 presidential campaign. Although there are no firm statistics, it is safe to assume that "Longhorns for Nixon" buttons were far more plentiful than were "Longhorns for McGovern" pins.

Associated Press sportswriter Denne H. Freeman wrote this history of the Longhorns in the mid-1970s. Beginning with the 1893 Thanksgiving Day game in Dallas, the book followed UT football up through the 1973 season.

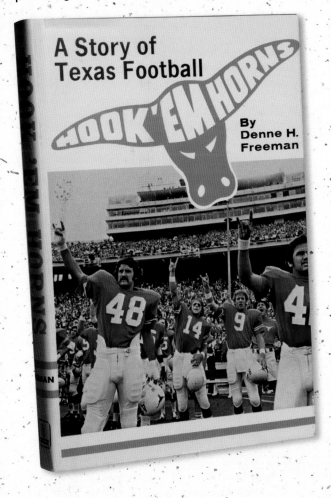

A Story of Texas Football
HOOK 'EM HORNS
By Denne H. Freeman

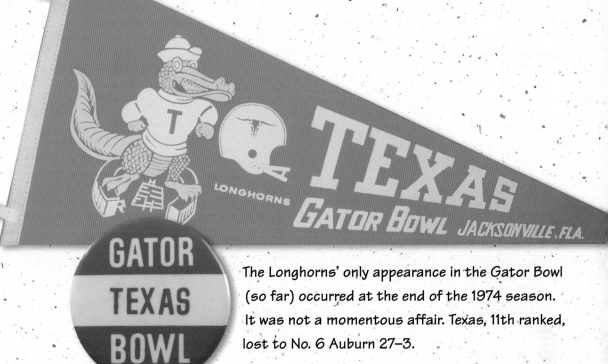

TEXAS
LONGHORNS
Gator Bowl JACKSONVILLE, FLA.

GATOR
TEXAS
BOWL

The Longhorns' only appearance in the Gator Bowl (so far) occurred at the end of the 1974 season. It was not a momentous affair. Texas, 11th ranked, lost to No. 6 Auburn 27–3.

This headline celebrates Texas's come-from-behind 17–13 win against Alabama in the 1973 Cotton Bowl.

San Antonio Light
FIRST IN TEXAS COMMUNITY SERVICE
Tuesday, January 2, 1973   1-C

Sports

Ostrum's For the Record .... Page 2-C
Mel Durslag's Column .... Page 3-C
Rodgers Stars in Orange Bowl .... Page 3-C
Charley Conerly's Analysis ...... Page 4-C
Scherwitz' Sportlights .... Page 5-C

Old Script Revived in Longhorns' Win

HARD-RUNNING Texas fullback Roosevelt Leaks (L) throws an elbow into the face of Alabama's Steve | Wade en route to an 11-yard gain in Cotton Bowl Classic. Longhorn coach Darrell Royal (C) is carried | off the field by his players after 17-13 win over Alabama and, at right, Texas quarterback Alan Lowry | is congratulated by teammate Don Crosslin after Lowry zipped 34 yards for winning TD in 4th quarter

Any Question About Number 0

Grasping for the Brass Ring

1977–1997

The 20 years of stability that Darrell Royal brought to Texas Longhorn football gave way to campaigns that always seemed to end just a little short of the goal—that reached for glory just as it floated away on the winds of time.

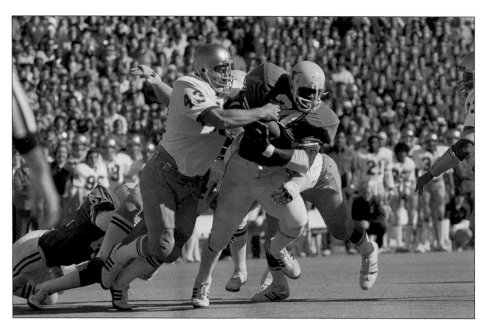

The Longhorns made it to the Cotton Bowl in 1977, their first post-Royal season. Here Heisman Trophy winner Earl Campbell fights for yardage against Notre Dame.

Opposite: *Considered the underdog against Nebraska, Texas came out the victor in 1996's first Big 12 championship, due partly to Derek Lewis's dramatic 61-yard pass reception late in the fourth quarter.*

Akers Comes to Texas

Fred Akers returned to Texas after two years coaching at Wyoming and came on strong. He didn't worry about replicating Darrell Royal's style, but his first team went undefeated in the regular season.

When Darrell Royal decided to leave coaching in 1976, there were three candidates for his job. Royal endorsed his longtime assistant Mike Campbell. The second candidate was Jim Wacker, the successful head coach at Texas Lutheran from 1971 to 1975. The third was Fred Akers, head coach at Wyoming, who had served on Royal's staff as an assistant from 1966 to 1974.

A native of Arkansas, Akers had played for the Razorbacks and served as a graduate assistant in Fayetteville for one season after finishing his playing career in 1959. A product of the Texas high school coaching ranks, Akers served as an assistant at Port Arthur and as head coach at Edinburg and Lubbock before Royal hired him to join the Texas staff in 1966.

At Texas, Akers had coached running backs and defensive backs. He was co-offensive coordinator prior to accepting the head coaching job at Wyoming in 1975. He took the Cowboys of Wyoming from 2–9 his first year to an 8–4 record and a Fiesta Bowl appearance in 1976.

Lorene Rogers, UT's president, was the nominal head of the search committee, but the real power belonged to Allan Shivers, chair of the UT Board of Regents. In the 1950s, Shivers served seven-and-a-half years as governor of Texas; by the 1970s, he was still one of the most powerful people in the state.

It was Shivers who decided that the next Texas Longhorn football coach would be Fred Akers. Akers was the antithesis of the laid-back Royal. Where Royal was comfortable in boots and jeans, Akers arrived for his first press conference nattily attired in a three-piece white suit.

Akers's youthful appearance and early success at Wyoming seemed to capture the attention of the decision makers, and he inherited a wealth of talent. With a crack new staff and a switch to the *I* formation to utilize the talents of eventual Heisman Trophy winner Earl Campbell, Akers burst onto the Texas scene in 1977.

His first team went 11–0 through the regular season, claimed the Southwest Conference championship, and spent the final half of the year atop the national polls. Only a loss in the Cotton Bowl Classic to Notre Dame denied Akers a national championship in his first season. He followed his spectacular start in 1977 with eight consecutive winning seasons and eight bowl berths, leading the Longhorns to national championship contention in 1977, 1981, and 1983.

Greatness in '77

Fred Akers arrived on the Austin UT campus with a wave of new enthusiasm, a superb coaching staff, and a football team ready to shed the memory of the disappointing, injury-riddled 1976 campaign. Despite a 5–5–1 finish and no bowl appearance in 1976, Texas began 1977 ranked No. 18 nationally. A 44–0 waxing of Boston College in the opener vaulted the team into the Top 10, at No. 9.

With eventual Heisman winner Earl Campbell leading the offense and the season's Outland Trophy winner, Brad Shearer, anchoring the defense, the Longhorns continued their march to a Top 5 ranking by crushing Virginia 68–0 and Rice 72–15.

They were No. 5 going into the fourth game of the season, but the annual showdown in Dallas with No. 2 Oklahoma loomed ahead. Texas hadn't beaten OU since 1970 and had only broken the Sooner winning streak with a gut-wrenching 6–6 tie in 1976.

The clash of the unbeatens in 1977 proved to be one of the classics of the historic series. Despite losing two quarterbacks to injury,

Texas prevailed 13–6, as Campbell shone offensively and future Hall of Famer Johnnie Johnson made a fourth-down stop to prevent a Sooner score late in the game.

From there, it was on to Arkansas, where the No. 2 ranked Longhorns came from behind to defeat the No. 8 Razorbacks 13–9. A week later, after mauling SMU, Texas ascended to the No. 1 spot in the country.

With Campbell joined by wide receivers Alfred Jackson and Johnny "Lam" Jones behind a powerful offensive line, Texas finished off the regular season with reserve quarterback Randy McEachern throwing four touchdown passes in a 57–28 thrashing of rival Texas A&M in College Station.

The dream season ended, however, with a 38–10 Cotton Bowl loss to Joe Montana's Notre Dame team. The No. 5 ranked Fighting Irish vaulted to the national championship, and the Longhorns, at 11–1, still finished a respectable No. 4 nationally.

The 1977 season was hard on Texas quarterbacks, but it didn't slow the team down. Below, fourth-string freshman QB Sam Ansley has just handed off to Earl Campbell.

McEachern's Miracle

Randy McEachern was an unlikely hero heading into the 1977 Texas-Oklahoma game. So unlikely, in fact, that the coaching staff considered keeping him off the travel squad.

McEachern was the third-string quarterback behind Mark McBath and strong-armed Jon Aune. With Earl Campbell at tailback and a pair of All-America–caliber wide receivers, calling plays for Texas seemed a simple task.

So when McBath went down with an ankle injury in the first quarter, Texas fans hardly stuttered. That faint stutter turned into a groan, however, as Jon Aune suffered a season-ending knee injury just before the first quarter ended.

It was then that Randy McEachern stepped onto the field at Cotton Bowl stadium and straight into Longhorn immortality. McEachern, who was slightly built, led Texas to a 13–6 victory over the Sooners. He followed that with a stellar performance in Fayetteville, Arkansas, and went on to quarterback Texas to a No. 1 regular-season ranking.

Even though injuries short-circuited McEachern's career during his 1978 senior campaign, he was later inducted into the Longhorn Hall of Honor.

The Longhorns' First Heisman

The massive football media guides produced by colleges today were only a dream in the late 1970s. The Longhorns' 1977 press guide was 4 inches by 9 inches—a pamphlet of 104 pages. Dressed in suits and looking all spiffed up, two men posed in the upper deck of Texas Memorial Stadium in the picture that graced the cover of the little book. The photo's caption read: "Head Coach Fred Akers, Heisman Trophy Candidate Earl Campbell."

Heisman candidate? That was a big stretch for a player who didn't even make the all-conference team the year before. Other teams were beginning the glitzy campaigns promoting candidates, but that single caption was the only published piece of literature proclaiming that Earl Campbell might be the best player in college football in 1977.

Campbell was famous long before he stepped onto the field to play football for Darrell Royal at Texas. His high school career in Tyler was the stuff from which legends are made. He was, to those who saw him, the greatest high school running back in state history.

Campbell's success at Texas was immediate in his freshman year of 1974. With All-America running back Roosevelt Leaks battling to come back from knee surgery, Campbell became the fullback in the Texas Wishbone. He gained 928 yards and helped lead the team to the Gator Bowl. As he prepared for a sophomore season where he would lead Texas to a Southwest Conference championship, he sat down for an interview.

"What makes you run?" he was asked.

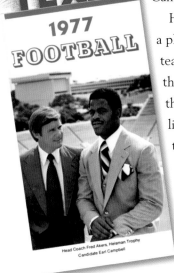

Above: *The bold but understated press guide.* **Right:** *Campbell carries the ball in the 1978 Cotton Bowl.*

"I want to be a pro football player. I want to be successful in what I try to do. The way I look at it, it's a gift that God gave me, and this is what I am meant to do. I want to make it so I can help take care of my family. I want to buy my Momma a house so she won't have to look at the stars at night through the holes in the roof. And after I have done that, maybe I can be of help to some who are less fortunate than I. I remember a sign in my high school dressing room that said, 'A quitter never wins, and a winner never quits.' I think about that all the time. There are times when I feel like I want to quit, but whenever I do, I just say a little prayer, and suddenly my day is brighter.

"If it weren't for the dark days, we wouldn't know what it is to walk in the light."

Campbell was named All-American that sophomore season, and then he struggled through 1976—Darrell Royal's last year—with a hamstring injury. In 1977, Earl set conference and school rushing records, leading the NCAA with 1,744 yards and 114 points.

While others were dancing and showboating after big plays, Coach Royal told Campbell, "Earl, when you get in that end zone, act like you have been there before."

And Earl was in there a lot. He led the 'Horns to an 11–0 record and a No. 1 ranking at the end of the regular season before they were met with the Notre Dame upset in the Cotton Bowl.

By the time Heisman votes were due, Campbell's story was on every magazine stand in the country. The prediction of that media guide came true: Campbell became the first Heisman Trophy winner in Texas Longhorn history.

His storied professional career created some of the most memorable plays the NFL had ever seen, as he ran his way into both the National Football Foundation's College Hall of Fame and the NFL Hall of Fame.

Momma's Roses

The most powerful person in Earl Campbell's life was his mother, Ann Campbell. After her husband died when Earl was only ten years old, she raised roses to earn the money to feed her 11 kids. Earl Campbell earned the nickname "The Tyler Rose" from his star turn at John Tyler High in Tyler and from his mother's hard work and sacrifice in raising him.

The recruiting of Earl Campbell in 1974 was a spirited competition. Ken Dabbs, a Texas assistant, was the point person for Darrell Royal's staff, and he was matched against the best recruiters from every school in the country. Many schools are alleged to have made illegal offers of payment to Campbell, which must have been a powerful temptation, but with the help and support of his mother, he stood firm and refused them.

"No," he would say defiantly, "my people have been bought and sold long enough."

In the spring of 1974, Earl Campbell signed to become a Texas Longhorn.

The Longhorns stirred a lot of hearts in 1977. It was their first real run at a national championship since their back-to-back wins in 1969 and '70.

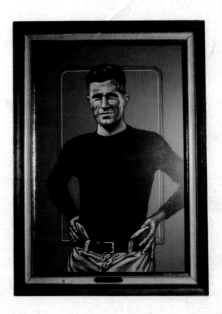

Razorback Football Illustrated
Saturday, October 15, 1977
Razorback Stadium

Official Game Program- $1.00

This license plate doesn't just identify the owner of a car—it announces the position the 'Horns held in the national polls for half of the '77 season.

Arkansas was ranked No. 8 when No. 2 Texas came to Fayetteville. The Longhorns triumphed 13–9 but remained at No. 2. A win over SMU the following week, however, pushed the team into the No. 1 spot, where it remained through the end of the season.

Earl Campbell's No. 20 jersey was retired by the University of Texas. In 1981, when Campbell starred with the Houston Oilers, the Texas legislature named him a state hero. He joined only Davy Crockett, Stephen F. Austin, and Sam Houston in that honor.

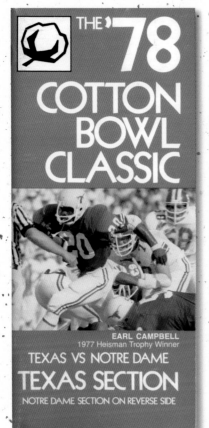

THE '78
COTTON BOWL CLASSIC

EARL CAMPBELL
1977 Heisman Trophy Winner
TEXAS VS NOTRE DAME
TEXAS SECTION
NOTRE DAME SECTION ON REVERSE SIDE

Entering the Cotton Bowl ranked No. 1, the Longhorns unfortunately had nowhere to go but down. Dreams of a fourth national championship were crushed by No. 5 Notre Dame, which took the title for itself by defeating Texas 38–10.

This vintage plastic Longhorn hat was once considered the height of fashion in certain circles.

The Need for Speed

Johnny "Lam" Jones still holds the Longhorn record for most receiving yards in a single game: 198 against Baylor in 1979.

On a late spring night in 1976, Johnny Jones ran his way into Texas high school sports immortality. A signee for Darrell Royal's Longhorn football program, he had already won both the 100-yard and 220-yard dashes at the University Interscholastic League State Meet. Lampasas, Jones's high school, needed to win the mile relay to claim the state AAA championship.

A slight wind stirred the banners in the infield and raised the flags at the south end of the track inside Texas Memorial Stadium. When Johnny Jones took the baton from the third runner for Lampasas, he was at least 50—and probably more like 75—yards behind the race's leading runner. In a burst of speed, he passed runners and steadily made up ground. By the last turn, he was within 10 yards of the lead. As the race's leader saw the tape at the finish line, he slid over to lane two, anticipating a win. But Johnny Jones gracefully ran past him in lane one, took the lead, broke the tape, and the rest was history. That summer, before Jones enrolled at the University of Texas, he was on the 1976 U.S. Olympic team, and his relay team won a gold medal in Montreal.

In Jones, Darrell Royal and Texas surely knew they were taking a chance. The Dallas Cowboys had previously gambled on a track star when they drafted Olympic gold medal sprinter "Bullet" Bob Hayes and turned him into a wide receiver. To Royal, Jones appeared to be Hayes's equal. Despite a disappointing 1976 season, "Lam" Jones (as he became known in order to differentiate him from Johnny Jones from Hamlin, who became "Ham") led the Longhorns in all-purpose yards.

In the spring of 1977, the young man who had finished sixth in the 100 meters in the Olympics won the Texas Relays in 9.85 seconds, a time that would have been a world record if the electronic clock had not malfunctioned. For the 1977 Longhorns football team, Lam moved to wide receiver under new head coach Fred Akers. He led Texas in receiving for three straight years, and in 1980, he was the first NFL draftee to receive a $1 million signing bonus.

Entering the '80s

It was Labor Day night, September 1, 1980. ABC Television, which had partnered with Texas and Arkansas to broadcast "made-for-TV" college football games in the past, decided to do it one more time. The network carrying the NCAA television package had hit the ratings jackpot in 1969, 1970, and 1976 by moving the game between the Razorbacks and the Longhorns to the end of the season.

For the 1980 season, network executives decided to go in another direction. They picked UT and Arkansas to kick off college football in the 1980s. During the course of the decade to come, which began with the Longhorns' 23–17 defeat of the Razorbacks at Texas Memorial Stadium, there would be many changes.

At Texas, Fred Akers was in his fourth season. The Longhorns had sniffed at a national championship in 1977 and won an impressive Sun Bowl victory over Maryland in 1978. Despite devastating injuries, only a loss to Texas A&M had kept them out of the Sugar Bowl in 1979.

Akers recruited an impressive pool of talented athletes for the Longhorns. Donnie Little, an excellent athlete who had been a star quarterback in high school, was the first African American quarterback in Texas history. But Little's presence was just one part of the stockpile of talent that Akers assembled after taking over a gifted group from Darrell Royal in 1977.

Even with all that talent, Texas was facing significant challenges as the clouds of recruiting improprieties over the Southwest Conference grew darker. In 1981, the Longhorns finished second in the country after representing the Southwest Conference in the Cotton Bowl Classic because

SMU was on probation. Over the next few years, nearly every team in the league would serve some kind of NCAA-mandated probation, with both SMU and TCU serving serious penalties—including the elimination of the Mustangs' football program for two years.

The 1980 NFL draft claimed seven Longhorns, including first-round choices Johnny "Lam" Jones, defensive backs Johnnie Johnson and Derrick Hatchett, and third-round pick defensive tackle Steve McMichael. That group paled considerably when compared with the 1982 draft, which had 12 Longhorns, and the 1984 record-setter, in which 17 Texas players were chosen.

Donnie Little blazed a trail as UT's first African American QB.

The biggest change of the decade, however, came from a court decision that was rendered in the summer of 1984. The universities of Georgia and Oklahoma had sued the NCAA, maintaining that the institutions should have the right to negotiate their own television contracts. When the courts ruled in their favor, the NCAA's control of televised college football was voided, and networks including ESPN offered a whole different deal to a brave new world of college athletics.

Flirting with No. 1

An opening 20–7 win against No. 5 Auburn demonstrated what Texas brought to the table in 1983. First-year running back Edwin Simmons loses a shoe but sidesteps a tackle.

Long before there was a Bowl Championship Series, the 1983 season produced the first clamor for play-offs in college football. Almost from the beginning of the season, the juggernauts of the game resided in the nation's midsection. But, by rule, they could never meet.

Nebraska, ranked No. 1 in the country, dominated the Big 8 Conference, while Texas, ranked No. 2, won all of its games in the Southwest Conference. The problem was that the winner of the Big 8—in this case Nebraska—was contractually bound to play in the Orange Bowl. By similar contractual obligation, the Southwest Conference champion, Texas, was obligated to play in the Cotton Bowl.

Fans and journalists alike demanded a meeting between the top two teams to decide the national championship. As the regular season neared an end, there was talk of a post-season game matching the two, but the NCAA quickly

discarded such overtures. Texas and Nebraska each continued to play well, and each believed that their team would eventually win the national championship.

Texas had opened the season ranked No. 3 and had convincingly disposed of No. 5 Auburn on Auburn's home field, 20–7. The next week, Texas was ranked No. 2. The Longhorns took out No. 8 Oklahoma 28–16 and then won a showdown for the Southwest Conference lead with No. 9 ranked SMU in Texas Stadium in Irving, 15–12.

With its wealth of talent, Texas was the first team since Army during World War II to have four first team All-Americans chosen by the Associated Press: Defensive backs Jerry Gray and Mossy Cade joined linebacker Jeff Leiding and offensive guard Doug Dawson on the elite squad. Nine players earned All–Southwest Conference honors.

Fans and media deemed both Nebraska and Texas invincible as the two schools finished their seasons unbeaten. In their final games, the Huskers beat Oklahoma, while Texas whipped Texas A&M 45–13. Nebraska headed to the Orange Bowl, where it was paired with Miami, while Texas faced off against No. 7 Georgia in the Cotton Bowl Classic. Texas and Georgia teed it up first, with Miami and the Cornhuskers slated for a night game in Miami.

Early in the 1983 campaign, Coach Akers had unleashed first-year running back Edwin Simmons, who seemed destined to become the next great Longhorn running back. Simmons rushed for 100 yards in the victory over Oklahoma in Dallas. Early in the first quarter in Arkansas the next week, he suffered an injury but limped off the field on his own power. That injury, however, was serious. Simmons was lost for the season, and he was never really effective again for the rest of his career.

The Longhorns thus became a team with a rock-solid defense and an efficient, if not overly productive, offense.

And so it was against the Bulldogs of Georgia in the Cotton Bowl. Freshman kicker Jeff Ward gave the Longhorns a 9–3 lead, and when UT stopped Georgia near mid-field late in the game, it appeared that No. 2 Texas led the chase for the national championship. But something went dreadfully wrong.

Anticipating a possible fake with less than three minutes left in the game, Texas failed to get its punt receiving team on the field, and a defensive back who caught the punt fumbled it. Georgia recovered, and the Bulldogs drove for the winning score, claiming a 10–9 victory.

That night after a late touchdown, Nebraska Coach Tom Osborne chose to go for two points rather than kick for a tie. The attempt failed, and Miami defeated the Cornhuskers. The Miami Hurricanes went on to receive the national championship trophy, Texas finished fifth nationally, and the dream game that never was . . . never was.

Seventeen seniors from the 1983 Texas Longhorns were drafted by the NFL, and several more signed as free agents, making it the largest draft class in Texas history. The next season, four more—including Lombardi winner Tony Degrate and All-America safety Jerry Gray—also entered the draft. Six more players from that team were drafted in 1986, so in all, more than 25 Longhorns from the 1983 team were drafted professionally.

For Akers, it was the third time in his seven years at Texas that one of his teams finished in the Top 5 nationally, and at that point his teams had won two SWC championships. But a disturbing trend was beginning to emerge: During those seven years, the Longhorns were only 2–5 in postseason bowl games.

Midway through the season, No. 9 SMU proved to be another victim of the Longhorn juggernaut that went undefeated but never rose above a No. 2 ranking.

Dodds Oversees Longhorn Excellence

In the spring of 1981, Bill Ellington was in his second year as the director of men's athletics at the University of Texas. At a routine meeting of the Athletics Council—an oversight body comprising faculty members and loyal supporters of the program—pressure was brought for Ellington to fire both football coach Fred Akers and basketball coach Abe Lemons.

"You have more problems than that," Ellington reportedly said, "because as of right now, I am retiring."

Ellington owned a small farm near Dallas, and he wasn't interested in fighting the politics of Texas athletics any longer. So he turned the program over to his only assistant, James Carroll "T" Jones, and took an extended vacation.

For the first time since UT had hired D. X. Bible in 1937, the university was officially looking for a director of athletics for its highly successful intercollegiate men's sports program. Jones, who had experience in the banking business as well as having been a football coach, had been with the program for only about 14 months. He was a candidate, but UT administration determined it needed a national search as well.

After a summer of searching, DeLoss Dodds, the athletics director at Kansas State University, was announced as the new Texas AD. Not everyone was certain that he was the right man for the job: The K-State football program was among the worst in the country, and Dodds took the brunt of several jokes.

To the surprise of many, however, Dodds turned ridicule into respect. The ninth AD in Texas history, Dodds went on to become the longest-serving, with a tenure of more than 25 years. Through new coaches, conference

changes, and a myriad of alterations on the landscape of college athletics, Dodds became not only a stabilizing factor but a force for change.

Under his watch, the Texas athletics program—both men's and women's—grew to be a $100-million business, and Dodds won every honor accorded his profession. Now one of the few collegiate programs that operates in the black financially, Texas has produced champions in every sport, and Dodds has also maintained an emphasis on success in the classroom. In addition, he has been a leader in the construction of new or remodeled facilities in all sports, which rank among the nation's best.

Dodds has certainly made his mark on UT athletics. Not only has Longhorn football prospered under his leadership, but Texas has won 12 national championships in three different sports since Dodds came on board.

Into the Valley

Seven years into the Fred Akers era at Texas, the coach had accumulated the highest percentage for a long-term coach in school history. The start of the 1984 season appeared to reflect even more success. The Longhorns—despite massive matriculation to the NFL from the 1983 team—beat Auburn and eventual Heisman Trophy winner Bo Jackson in the season opener and then knocked off Penn State at the Meadowlands 28–3.

By the third game of the season, Texas had a No. 1 ranking. A 15–15 tie with Oklahoma dropped UT from the top spot, but two games later, the Longhorns were back to No. 2, with a 5–0–1 record. The season began to unravel, however, with a loss to Houston, and Texas dropped four of its last five games—which included an embarrassing 55–17 loss to Iowa in the first-ever Freedom Bowl in Anaheim, California.

The 1984 season saw a free-for-all in college sports television negotiations, and the Longhorns took advantage of it, appearing on TV a record nine times. In the end, the broadcasts weren't pretty, as Texas suffered through loss after loss.

But by 1985, the landscape of college football had changed dramatically. Oklahoma was in competition for the national championship in the Associated Press poll and came out on top. Jackie Sherrill transformed his Texas A&M program into contention, and SMU was riding a strong wave, though NCAA investigations were closing in on the Ponies' program.

Even as Akers's Longhorns finished the regular season 8–3, unrest mounted among UT football supporters, who were calling for the coach's termination. Though Texas was unranked at the end of the season, the firestorm surrounding the Forty Acres grew when they fell to No. 11 ranked Air Force in the Bluebonnet Bowl.

Akers made staff changes in the off-season, but an uncommon number of injuries plagued the 1986 team. And when Texas lost its final regular season game in Austin to rival Texas A&M, Akers earned his first losing record at 5–6. More importantly, it was Texas's first losing record in 30 years—and it was enough to end Akers's tenure. He departed with a record of 86–31–2, second only to Darrell Royal in both total victories and winning percentage.

Texas made a good showing of its dominance against the Nittany Lions, upping its ranking from No. 2 to No. 1. Alas, that kind of power wouldn't last as the '84 season continued.

Linebacker Duane Duncum and defensive end Thomas Aldridge go in against the Sooners in 1986, but their effort is not enough to prevent a 47–12 loss.

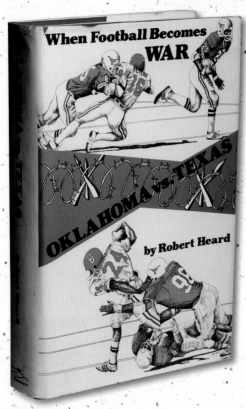

This leather belt buckle commemorates 100 years since classes first began on the Austin campus of the University of Texas.

A 13–7 win over No. 14 SMU in 1984 pushed the Longhorns' national ranking from No. 3 to No. 2. Texas couldn't retain its momentum, however, and the end of the season saw the team tied for third place in the Southwest Conference.

Robert Heard's 544-page examination of the UT-OU rivalry burst upon the world in 1980. Heard has described the Texas-Oklahoma rivalry as the "meanest and most bitter in the country."

Were drinks actually colder when they came out of a Texas Longhorns ice chest? No one can say for sure, but they certainly seemed to be more satisfying.

Sports Section B

Local, State, World Sports

Page 1

Sports — Phone 744-3611

Saturday Morning, January 2, 1982

Longhorns maintain jinx over Alabama

Pupil, tutor face in Buc-Bulldog tilt

By SCOTT ROTHSCHILD
News Sports Writer

Tonight's O'Connell-Hitchcock basketball game features a coaching matchup that could only raise the temperature to this already hotly-contested area rivalry.

O'Connell coach Ken Wilkins will lead the Buccaneers against the Bulldogs — a team headed by Wilkins' former high school mentor, Gary Crowell.

The game will mark the first time either of these men have coached against one another.

Under the tutelage of Crowell, Wilkins earned district most valuable player honors in 1976 by pacing the Bulldogs to a bi-district championship.

"He's one of the finest young men I've ever coached," Crowell said. "I'd like to see him win all of his games, except against me."

After graduating from Hitchcock, Wilkins played college ball at Panola and then later at St. Edward's University.

The second-year O'Connell coach admitted the game — which will tipoff at 7:30 p.m. at O'Connell — "will be like coming home."

In more ways than one.

The Bucs' game-plan is an almost carbon copy of Hitchcock's. Last season, Wilkins incorporated Crowell's playbook at Pearland in the O'Connell squad.

"We do similar things," Crowell said. "It's an honor to have someone who played under you to use your ideas."

"Still, I'm sure he (Wilkins) would like to beat his old coach," Crowell added.

Although the Bucs suffered through a dreary 2-23 campaign in 1980, O'Connell is off to a fine 9-5 start this season.

Brewer-led rally sparks Texas to Cotton Bowl win

DALLAS (AP) — Sophomore tailback Terry Orr dashed 8 yards for a touchdown with 2:05 left to cap a Robert Brewer-led comeback as No.6 Texas maintained its jinx over No.3 Alabama with a 14-12 victory in the 46th annual Cotton Bowl Friday.

Brewer, starting only his fourth game of the season for the Longhorns, scampered 30-yards for a touchdown on a quarterback draw with 10:22 to go in the game.

After an Alabama punt, Brewer ignited the Longhorns to a touchdown in 11 plays covering 80 yards.

He completed a third-down pass of 37 yards to tight end Lawrence Sampleton to keep the drive alive and connected on three other passes, including a 19-yarder to Donnie Little, to set up the game-winning touchdown.

Alabama led 10-0 on a 6-yard touchdown pass from quarterback Walter Lewis to Jesse Bendross and Peter Kim's 24-yard field goal.

Alabama's Joey Jones returned Texas' kickoff a Cotton Bowl-record 61 yards after the second Longhorn touchdown, but William Graham intercepted a Lewis pass on the Texas 1-yard line with 1:47 to go.

Punter John Goodson then took a deliberate safety with 48 seconds remaining so the Longhorns wouldn't have to risk getting a kick blocked.

Alabama then got the ball back with 43 seconds to play on its own 41 on the free kick after the safety. But Lewis was trapped twice trying to pass and time ran out on the Crimson Tide.

Texas finished Texas' record to 10-1-1 and Alabama's at 9-2-1. It was the new NCAA

Bryant from adding the 316th victory to his record for college head coaches.

But it kept alive Texas' streak of never having lost to the Crimson Tide, who finished the year at 9-2-1. Texas is now 7-0-1 against the Southeast Conference Crimson Tide.

The loss shut down Alabama's outside chance for a shot at the national championship.

A sellout crowd of 73,243 watched the frenzied affair in 50-degree weather.

Alabama charged up and down the field in the first half but could only post one touchdown. Starting quarterback Alan Gray fumbled away to Texas tackle Ralph Darnell on the Longhorn 19 to end one promising Alabama drive. After a scoreless first quarter, Alabama stormed 82 yards in 7 plays behind backup quarterback Lewis.

Lewis scrambled for 17 yards and halfback Joe Carter dashed 14 yards before Lewis whipped a 37-yard completion to tight end Bart Krout on the Longhorn 12.

On third and 4 from the Texas 6, Lewis rolled to his right, dodged a tackler, and floated a touchdown pass to Bendross, who was wide open after defender Graham fell down.

Texas threatened twice in the first half. Brewer was sacked on 3rd and 5 from the Alabama 39, by tackle Jackie Cline to spoil one drive.

Defensive end Russ Wood of the Tide shortcircuited the other threat by sacking Brewer on 3rd and 10 from the Tide 27. Raul Allegre's 50-yard field-goal attempt against a light mph wind fell short.

Tide QB Alan Gray (14) scrambles away from Texas safety Bobby Johnson

Warner directs Lions

The Longhorns capped their 1981 season with a 14–12 Cotton Bowl victory over Alabama.

TEXAS vs. GEORGIA

The 1984 Cotton Bowl Classic

Texas was unbeaten going into the 1984 Cotton Bowl against the Georgia Bulldogs, but a disastrous error late in the game led to a 10–9 loss. It was Akers's second in a string of four bowl-game losses, which ultimately caused the UT faithful to rethink their loyalty to him.

FREEDOM BOWL

IOWA HAWKEYES VS. **TEXAS LONGHORNS**

ANAHEIM STADIUM ★ ANAHEIM, CALIFORNIA

THE OFFICIAL COMMEMORATIVE MAGAZINE

The first annual Freedom Bowl in Anaheim did not exactly serve as a showplace for the best of Longhorn football. The 1984 season was becoming more and more of a disappointment, but no one was ready for a rain-soaked 55–17 loss to Iowa. It was the third of Akers's four straight bowl losses.

The Homecoming

During Fred Akers's reign as football coach, the Longhorn nation was fractured. Akers had the unenviable task of following in the footsteps of legendary coach Darrell Royal. Compounding the problem Akers faced, Royal had made it obvious on his retirement that he had wanted to turn the program over to his long-time assistant, Mike Campbell. So when Akers stumbled with the losing 1986 season, that was all it took to begin the search for a new head coach.

DeLoss Dodds, in his fifth year as Texas athletics director, began a national search, but it was clear from the start that, as far as the Royal loyalists were concerned, that search needed to go no farther than to Lubbock, Texas, where David McWilliams had just completed his first season as the Red Raider football coach.

McWilliams was a tri-captain on Texas's first national champion team in 1963. He coached in high school for a few years and then returned to UT as an assistant coach in 1970. Working first for Royal and

then for Akers, he logged 16 years as an assistant before taking the job at Texas Tech in 1986, where he led the Red Raiders to a bowl appearance in his first season.

The timing was far from perfect, as McWilliams had only one year of collegiate head-coaching experience and, in fact, had only been away from the Longhorn football program for that one year. But Texas was searching for the next Darrell Royal—a homespun coach who could unite the Texas team and fans. McWilliams seemed to fit the bill perfectly. As the new head coach of the Longhorns, McWilliams gained the support and guidance of Darrell Royal and Mike Campbell, who served in an advisory capacity to the new coaching staff. The players, however, were another story.

In the latter Akers years, recruiting had declined. At one point, even loyal Texas fans advised recruits not to come, largely because most schools in the Southwestern Conference were either under investigation or already on probation for NCAA recruiting violations. McWilliams inherited

David McWilliams, a former Longhorn player and assistant coach, was welcomed back to Austin after proving his mettle in his first year as head coach at Texas Tech.

a few superstars, but depth was a serious question as he embarked on his inaugural season in 1987.

Though the Longhorns finished 1987 with a decent 7–5 record, the thrilling season was a delight for fans. First, there was a stunning victory over No. 15 Arkansas. Trailing 14–10 with only 1:48 remaining in the game, Texas quarterback Bret Stafford maneuvered the Longhorns from their 44 to the Arkansas 18-yard line. As time expired, Stafford connected with receiver Tony Jones in the end zone for a 16–14 victory—the first time in its storied history that Texas won a game on the final play. Texas closed out the season with a 32–27 victory over unranked Pittsburgh in the Bluebonnet Bowl. With a brilliant performance, tailback Eric Metcalf thrust himself into the 1988 Heisman Trophy race.

Above and right: *Eric Metcalf still holds UT records for career receptions by a running back (125) and receptions by a running back in a single season (42, in 1986 and '88). He was a first-round draft pick for the Cleveland Browns in 1989.*

Unfortunately, the next season turned disastrous for the Longhorns. Metcalf missed the first game of the season because of a clerical snafu that resulted in an NCAA one-game penalty. The Longhorns lost six of their last seven games to finish 4–7—the worst record for a Texas team since 1956.

In 1990, Texas seemed to turn the corner. The Longhorns won the Southwest Conference and finished 10–2 on the year. By the time they played Miami in the Cotton Bowl Classic, the 'Horns were ranked No. 3 in the nation—the first time they had been ranked in the Top 10 at the end of regular season play since 1983. McWilliams was given a new five-year contract at the end of that season in appreciation.

Shock the Nation

The University of Texas had nearly disappeared from the national collegiate football landscape when the 1990 season began. The Longhorns were coming off of back-to-back losing seasons, so when Texas journeyed to Penn State for the opener, it was expected to be merely a footnote among the day's games. But the Longhorns batted down the Nittany Lions' final pass attempt to cap a surprising 17–13 victory.

Upon entering the dressing room after the game, one exuberant Longhorn proclaimed, "We're gonna shock the nation!"

Thus, Texas's 1990 "Shock the Nation" tour began.

For the rest of the regular season, the Longhorns lost only one game—to eventual co–national champion Colorado. They took down No. 4 ranked Oklahoma and defeated No. 3 rated Houston. In all, five of their opponents were nationally ranked. Texas finished the season with a 28–27 triumph over rival Texas A&M, snapping an Aggie winning streak that dated back to 1984.

The "Tour" ended on a frigid day in Dallas, when defending national champion Miami, ranked No. 4 nationally, defeated the No. 3 Horns 46–3.

Adrian Walker's 88-yard kickoff return led off the third quarter against Penn State and set up a 6-yard touchdown by Chris Samuels on the next play. That provided the 'Horns their first lead of the game, and Texas never looked back.

John Mackovic: A New Direction

Mackovic was chosen for his attention to offense, but defense suffered under his tenure.

Even though David McWilliams had been awarded a five-year contract in 1990, a disappointing 1991—which saw the Longhorns finish with their third losing record (5–6) in his five-year tenure—brought the McWilliams era to an abrupt end. He was reassigned as head of the Texas Letter-Winners Association and closed his Texas coaching career with a 31–26 record.

Thus Texas embarked on the search for its third head coach in the 15 years since Darrell Royal's resignation. After years of homegrown products with Texas connections, it was time for the Longhorns to search nationally for the new coach.

For 35 years, since Royal first walked the sidelines in burnt orange, his influence had reigned over the program. Fred Akers, even though he wasn't Royal's personal pick, coached as an assistant with Royal for almost ten years, and McWilliams's well-documented tenure included playing and coaching under Royal.

Texas scoured the nation for an experienced head coach who was also considered an offensive-minded specialist. The Longhorns ended their search by hiring John Mackovic, who was the head coach and athletics director at the University of Illinois. Mackovic was not only credited with the rebirth of the Illini program, but he had been the youngest head coach in professional football when he served with the Kansas City Chiefs. Even more, Mackovic had cultivated a good reputation in Texas as the Dallas Cowboys' quarterbacks coach under Tom Landry.

The introduction of Mackovic as the Longhorns' new head coach came in the classy Bass Concert Hall of the Performing Arts Center on the UT campus, and in a way it was prophetic: Mackovic was presented onstage, separated from the media and fans by the wide chasm of the orchestra pit. Where McWilliams was folksy, Mackovic had a demeanor more suited to a corporate CEO. If McWilliams was a burger and a beer, Mackovic was fine wine and pine nuts. As one prominent media member wrote, "Texas is used to John Wayne, and they have just hired David Niven."

John Mackovic came into a program that had really changed little in 25 years. Facilities that had been state of the art in 1972 were in need of significant repair in 1992. Mackovic didn't hesitate to voice his opinion, though his words dealt a blow to the pride of the Longhorns.

"Change," he said at the time, "has no constituency."

The next few years proved him right.

North vs. South

Priest Holmes soars through the air against North Carolina in the 1994 Sun Bowl. He ran for four of the Longhorns' five touchdowns, helping his team to a come-from-behind 35–31 win.

The dawning of the Big 12 Conference was a gradual process that began in the early 1990s and culminated with the conference's inaugural season in 1996. In terms of national stature, the Big 8 Conference dominated the Southwest Conference before the two were joined to form the Big 12.

So when founders divided the league into two parts—with Nebraska, Colorado, Kansas, Kansas State, Missouri, and Iowa State in the North Division and Texas, Texas A&M, Texas Tech, Baylor, Oklahoma, and Oklahoma State in the South Division—the advantage appeared to be with the northern schools. Never was that difference more evident than in the first-ever Big 12 championship game, which was between UT and Nebraska.

Texas was a season removed from the final Southwest Conference championship when, as part of the Bowl Alliance, the Longhorns played in the 1995 Sugar Bowl. In 1996, the Longhorns were 7–4 overall in the regular season, with a winning 6–2 conference record.

Nebraska, on the other hand, triumphed as one of two (along with Florida State) "teams of the '90s." The two-time defending national champions swept the North Division in 1996 with an 8–0 league record and were ranked No. 3 with a 10–1 overall record when they headed to St. Louis for the Big 12 Championship. Oddsmakers installed the Cornhuskers as 21-point favorites.

Meanwhile, John Mackovic's Texas program had not endeared itself to the Longhorn faithful. The coach's first two seasons resulted in records of 6–5 and 5–5–1, and there was unrest among the fans. When his 1994 team was crushed by rival Texas A&M 34–10 to mark a 5–4 record with two games

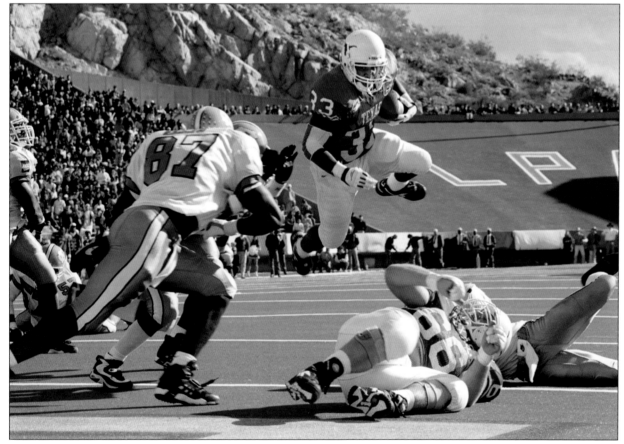

left to play, the support base neared a revolt. Luckily, a young redshirt quarterback named James Brown rose to the occasion.

Brown, who was given a shot against Oklahoma because regular Longhorn signal caller Shea Morenz was injured, led Texas to back-to-back victories (including an impressive 63–35 win over Baylor) to end the regular season. Then, with Mackovic's job hanging in the balance, Texas beat North Carolina in the Sun Bowl 35–31, ending the season at a respectable 8–4.

Even though Texas finished the 1995 season at 10–2–1, a 55–27 loss at Notre Dame rendered the 'Horns "not ready for prime time" in the minds of many fans. Still, they appeared in 1996 to represent the Big 12 South in the league's first championship game.

Nebraska, No. 3, was heavily favored to win—the Longhorns weren't even nationally ranked, after all——but Texas scored first and, even as the lead went back and forth, always stayed close. The game turned on a dramatic fourth-down call by Mackovic. Texas, clinging to a three-point lead at its own 28-yard line with 2:40 remaining, faced fourth down and inches. Instead of punting, Mackovic decided to go for it. The plan worked, and Texas won 37–27. The coach was the toast of Texas as fans celebrated his gutsy call. The win earned the 'Horns a berth in the Bowl Alliance against Penn State in the Fiesta Bowl, where a strong Nittany Lion second half resulted in UT's fifth loss in an 8–5 season.

Mackovic's 1996 glory was short-lived. The 1997 season began with high hopes, but when the Longhorns lost to UCLA by a score of 66–3 in the season's second game, Mackovic's fate was sealed. His final year ended with a 4–7 record, and once again, Texas began looking for a new coach.

James Brown, Priest Holmes, and the Miracle in St. Louis

When a reporter questioned Texas quarterback James Brown's confidence before the first-ever Big 12 Championship and pointed out that the Longhorns were 21-point underdogs to Nebraska, Brown fired back. "Hey, I don't pay attention to that. We might even win," he said.

Brown made his prediction come true—with a little help from his friends.

He completed 19 passes for 353 yards, but the real surprise of the game was running back Priest Holmes, who collected 120 rushing yards and three touchdowns. Holmes went on to become the leading rusher in the history of the NFL's Kansas City Chiefs.

Brown's biggest moment of the game came in the fourth quarter as the team faced fourth and inches from its own 28 with 2:40 remaining. Coach Mackovic had given him a play called "Steelers roll left," a run-pass option, and as the Longhorns broke the huddle, Brown warned tight end Derek Lewis: "Be ready." "For what?" Lewis replied. "I just might throw it," said Brown.

Brown rolled left, pulled up, and tossed a short pass to Lewis, who caught it and took it to the Nebraska 11-yard line. On the next play, Holmes scored the final touchdown for a 37–27 victory.

TEXAS MEMORIES

Texas fans came up with this variation on the "We're number 1" foam finger. Nothing says "Hook 'em, Horns" like a raised foam index finger and pinky in burnt orange.

The holder of this ticket saw an exciting finish to the game. The Longhorns seemed safely ahead, scoring a touchdown in each of the first three quarters with no response from SMU. The Mustangs got on the board just before the end of the third quarter and had a 17-point fourth to pull even with a tie. A 40-yard field goal with 16 seconds on the clock sealed the deal for UT, 27–24.

SAT., OCT. 25, 1986
MEMORIAL STADIUM · AUSTIN, TEXAS

GAME 3 $15.00
SMU   NO EXCHANGE
                NO REFUND

ENTER GATE   5 OR 6

032	21	03
SEC.	ROW	SEAT

A win against the Sooners is always gratifying, and in 1989, David McWilliams oversaw the first Longhorn victory since 1983.

The Paris News

Section B

Page 1B

Sports

The Paris News, Sun., Oct. 15, 1989

Longhorns stun OU with final TD, 28-24

☐ Walker catches winning pass with 93 ticks left

By The Associated Press

DALLAS — Texas started an all-freshmen backfield and was an 15-point underdog to 15th-ranked Oklahoma. Yet it was the Longhorns' fans who tore down a goal post and carried coach David McWilliams off the field.

Texas' 28-24 victory Saturday on Peter Gardere's 25-yard touchdown pass to Johnny Walker with 93 seconds to play was as unlikely as any upset in the 84-year history of the annual Red River rivalry.

The Longhorns hadn't won over Oklahoma since 1983 and barely beat Rice 31-30 last week on a controversial touchdown.

"We got to do it, and we have got to have the TD," Gardere said in the huddle before the 66-yard game winning drive. "It's been a long time since we beat them. Let's do it now."

It was the first time Texas' seniors had defeated the Sooners. Texas coach David McWilliams said he thought Gardere had overthrown Walker.

"Somehow he came down with the ball," McWilliams said. "Well, we finally beat Oklahoma. This means we can turn things around and be a good team. I think the team knows now what it takes to be a champion."

McWilliams, savoring his first win as a coach over the Sooners, said: "I was nervous when Oklahoma went ahead late, but Peter kept his poise and made some great throws. It was just a tremendous performance."

Gardere didn't earn a starting job for the 'Horns until last week against Rice.

Oklahoma coach Gary Gibbs gave Texas a pat on the back for its rally.

"I give Texas credit for the way they came out and played," he said. "For the most part, we dominated the second half until their final drive."

Gibbs, Oklahoma's former defensive coordinator, was attempting to

win his first game against Texas since Switzer retired.

"After the game, I told our players that I still had confidence in them and that if we continue to improve we will become a good football team," Gibbs said.

Running back Ike Lewis said: "Texas was fired up and ready. No one likes to lose, especially a game like this."

Oklahoma quarterback Tink Collins said even after the Sooners scored a go-ahead touchdown with three minutes to play, he knew the game was still on.

"I knew it wasn't over," he said. "Texas was able to move the ball early in the game, so I figured they could do it again. I hoped our defense could hold them. They couldn't."

Oklahoma quarterback Tink Collins hit Arthur Guess with a 41-yard scoring pass to bring the Sooners within 21-14. A 30-yard field goal by R.D. Lasher narrowed the margin to 21-17.

Then Lewis scored again to seemingly clinch another Sooner victory before Gardere's heroics.

IN FOR SIX: Texas wide receiver Tony Jones (4) pulls down a pass in the end zone for a touchdown in the first quarter as Oklahoma defensive back Charles Franks (15) reaches for him. The Longhorns stunned the Sooners, 28-24.

Photo by AP

Stewart, A's shut out SF in 1st game

By The Associated Press

OAKLAND, Calif. — This time, Dave Stewart finished what he started. And this time, the Oakland Athletics didn't need to worry about

MP topples Pantherettes

From Staff Reports

MOUNT PLEASANT — Playing good enough for the

Artist Gary Patterson is known for his humorous illustrations of sports and other subjects. This plate features his take on the cool, collected Longhorns fan.

Fred Akers was not the most popular man on campus in 1986. Bringing the 'Horns in with a losing 5–6 record was all many boosters needed to know to start looking for a new coach. David McWilliams, who had been Akers's assistant the year before, seemed to be what the fans were looking for.

Stunning nearly everyone, the unranked Longhorns rolled over the No. 3 ranked Nebraska Cornhuskers 37–27 in 1996 to become the first Big 12 champions.

David McWilliams coached the Longhorns against the Sooners for the first time in 1987. His team was still getting its bearings with its new coach, however, and lost 44–9 against the top-ranked team in the country.

Mack Brown's in Town

1998–Today

For more than 20 years, Texas searched for a winning coach as beloved as Darrell Royal. That search ended with Mack Brown. Born in the foothills of Tennessee and possessing a quick country wit, Brown was etched with character and integrity. Mack Brown's goal for the Longhorns was to "win championships with nice kids who graduate."

The 2005 season once again saw the Longhorns on top with a national championship. Mack Brown waves "Hook 'em, Horns" as he receives the championship trophy after defeating USC 41–38 in the Rose Bowl.

Quarterback Vince Young tagged tight end David Thomas (16) for ten receptions and 88 yards in his Rose Bowl performance. Here Thomas seems to glide through the air after snagging one of Young's passes.

Brown Arrives in Austin

University of North Carolina Head Coach Mack Brown had heard the rumors: John Mackovic was on his way out as the head coach of the Texas Longhorns, and a deal seemed sealed for the Longhorns to hire a coach from the Big Ten to replace him.

When Brown was asked to interview for the job, he nearly declined. Eventually, he agreed to meet with members of the Texas search committee during a trip to Atlanta for an Atlantic Coast Conference academic banquet. With his wife, Sally, by his side, Brown attended the meeting that changed the course of Longhorn football.

In many ways, Brown's coming to Texas was a long shot. He had achieved national status leading the North Carolina football program, and Sally Brown was firmly established as a successful land developer in the Triangle area of Raleigh, Durham, and Chapel Hill. But one thing that Texas had in its favor was Mack Brown's respect for the history and tradition of Longhorn football. Growing up in Cookeville, Tennessee, in the 1960s, Brown had watched Texas football with his father and grandfather, both of whom were coaches. As a youngster, he'd admired the prominent coaches of the day—including Darrell Royal.

So when Brown learned that Royal would be accompanying the search committee to Atlanta, he was pleased. During the interview at the Four Seasons Hotel, both Mack and Sally Brown impressed the committee to such an extent that the UNC coach instantly became many members' first choice. The committee went from interest to urgency in its pursuit of Mack Brown.

"When we put everything we wanted in a coach together," said one committee member, "he was all of that—and more."

Mack Brown had played college football at Vanderbilt and Florida State and had begun his coaching career as an assistant at Southern Mississippi. In 1983, at 32, he spent a year as head coach at Appalachian State. After a successful season there,

Although Brown seemed to start slow, winning only one of his first three games as head coach, the Longhorns ended the 1998 season with a 9–3 record and a No. 15 ranking.

he moved to Oklahoma, where for one year he served as the offensive coordinator for Barry Switzer's Sooners. In 1985, he returned to head coaching, this time as head coach and athletics director at Tulane University. He moved to North Carolina in 1987, where he took the football program to its greatest success in the seasons prior to his interview with the Texas committee.

Brown had a certain charm that reflected the wit and wisdom Texas fans had seen in Royal so many years earlier. At North Carolina, he'd achieved a lettered-athlete graduation rate of 70 percent, sent players to the NFL, and battled competitively against ACC kingpin Florida State, which boasted one of the 1990s' most successful programs in the country.

The Texas committee's decision to pick Brown was easy; Brown's decision to accept was much harder. After the interview in Atlanta, Mack and Sally Brown returned to North Carolina to weigh their options. After a sleepless night and meetings with North Carolina administrators, the Browns decided to come to Texas.

As Sally Brown put it, "We weren't leaving North Carolina . . . we were going to Texas."

And so, late on the night of December 3, 1997, Mack Brown—still wearing a blue-patterned Carolina sweater—walked into the football team meeting room of the soon-to-be remodeled Moncrief-Neuhaus Center at Darrell K Royal–Texas Memorial Stadium. There, just hours after

his tearful goodbye to the Tar Heels of Carolina in Chapel Hill, Brown met his new football team. From the outset, Brown inspired them: He built camaraderie by telling them they were all in it together; he shared their pain at losing a coach; he sympathized with them for taking the brunt of fan and media criticism after a disappointing season. The next season would be different, he told them. He wouldn't wait to rebuild; for the sake of the seniors, and the rest of the team, he wanted to win right away.

The following day, at a press conference attended by more than 500 people, Brown sat at a podium with his wife and DeLoss Dodds and was introduced as the new head football coach of the Texas Longhorns. Afterward, he posed for pictures in front of a burnt-orange Texas banner. He shook hands and posed with the man into whose large shadow he was about to step: Darrell Royal.

Hook 'em, Horns! One of Mack Brown's first lessons to the Longhorns was to display their pride in their school and their team.

Williams Runs Away with the '98 Season

During his junior year of 1997, despite playing on a team that finished 4–7, star Longhorn running back Ricky Williams won the Doak Walker Trophy. In the glow of his impressive win, Williams had to decide whether to return for his senior season or declare himself eligible for the NFL draft.

The relationship between Williams and Coach Mack Brown had initially been a clash of contrasting personalities and backgrounds. Ricky Williams was a California kid, complete with dreadlocks and a strong admiration for reggae singer Bob Marley. Mack Brown was a country boy from Tennessee. He believed that every appearance a player made on the field was a job interview, and therefore, he enforced a "no facial hair, no jewelry" policy. During a private meeting, Brown told Williams that he would have to cut off his beloved dreadlocks.

That edict could have been a deal-breaker had Williams not met Mack and Sally Brown for lunch the next day. During that meal, he saw a family atmosphere in the way the Browns interacted with each other. It also didn't hurt that Brown promised Williams that the team would have a strong defense and that he would let Williams run the ball.

Still undecided, Williams went home to California. En route, he made the decision that would change the look of Longhorn football and set the course for Mack Brown's first team at Texas: He decided to return for his senior season.

Williams impressed Brown by asking if the team was disciplined enough to win. "He didn't ask me if he could set records or win the Heisman Trophy. He wanted to know how our team would play defense and if we had a chance to be good," Brown recalled.

Brown learned something else in the bargain. "I have always believed that, like it or not, the public is wary of folks who look different, and Ricky looked different. But I quickly found out that Ricky wasn't wearing his hair in dreadlocks to make a statement. He just liked his hair in dreadlocks.

Williams rolled over Rice, rushing for 318 yards and six touchdowns in the 59–21 Longhorn victory.

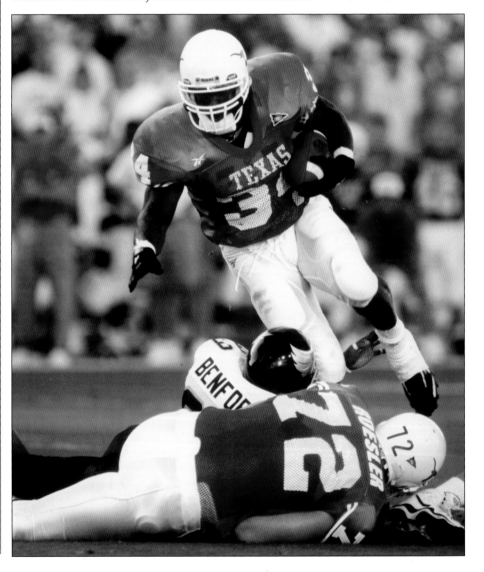

Ricky Williams wore Doak Walker's No. 37 in the 1998 Texas-Oklahoma match-up at the Cotton Bowl in tribute to the football giant's own achievements in that stadium with SMU.

His hair became his trademark, and it wasn't likely that Ricky would need to interview for jobs. A lot of people were telling Ricky to take the money and leave school. So as our relationship grew, I was greatly complimented when he asked me a critical question: 'Should I do what everybody tells me I should do, or should I do what I want to do?' he asked."

Brown advised Williams, "Few people in life ever get to do what they really want to do. If you need the money right now, then you should go. If you don't, then do whatever it is that you really want to do."

Thus began the incredible 1998 season. After losing two of its first three games, Texas rebounded to finish 9–3. Williams won the Heisman Trophy by one of the largest margins in history. He also set NCAA career records for rushing, 6,279 yards, and total yardage, 7,206. His single best game was against Iowa State on October 3, 1998: Williams rushed for 350 yards and had total yardage of 367 (Texas won 54–33). In 1978, he rushed for 2,124 yards and accumulated 2,386 yards total. Ricky Williams finished his college career with 21 NCAA records and 46 UT records.

When he won his first Doak Walker Trophy as a junior, Williams bonded with Walker himself, who was critically injured in a skiing accident shortly thereafter. When Walker died from complications following the injury, Ricky Williams honored his friend by wearing a No. 37 jersey during the Texas-Oklahoma game at the Cotton Bowl—known as "The House that Doak Built."

To honor Williams after his record-setting final game with Texas A&M, Heisman winners Earl Campbell, Tony Dorsett, and legendary Aggie John David Crow joined him on the field for postgame activities.

Validation

The 1998 season marked not only a Heisman Trophy run for Longhorn Ricky Williams, it gave Mack Brown's program instant credibility on the national scene. And no game meant more to that image than the Longhorns' 20–16 victory over No. 7 Nebraska in Lincoln.

The Cornhuskers were riding a 47-game winning streak at home, and their famed "Blackshirt" defense accepted the challenge of facing Williams, who was one of the leading candidates to win the Heisman. In a war of words before the game, Nebraska's defenders made it clear that they intended to hold Williams to fewer than 100 yards. In a televised interview the day

of the game, the usually subdued Williams accepted the challenge, saying, "They are going to have to stop us."

In the end, Williams carried the ball 37 times and rushed for 150 yards. After the Texas victory, the Nebraska crowd stood and applauded, chanting "Heisman" as Williams left the field with Mack Brown.

The Stadium Grows Again

Not since 1972, when the west-side upper deck was completed, had there been significant additions to Darrell K Royal–Texas Memorial Stadium's seating capacity. But in 1998, big changes were afoot.

After the final game of the 1997 football season, construction began on a 5,000-seat upper deck on the stadium's east side. The new deck included 52 stadium suites. This was only one phase of the massive construction project, which was approved in 1996 and had been in the planning stages for two years.

Texas Memorial Stadium was renamed to honor legendary coach Darrell Royal, becoming Darrell K Royal–Texas Memorial Stadium in 1996. The artificial turf, which had been installed in 1969, was removed in favor of natural grass. That field was christened Joe Jamail Field in honor of the prominent UT supporter whose gift made it possible.

At the same time, extensive remodeling was completed on the football facility at the stadium's south end. The facility's new name was Moncrief-Neuhaus Athletics Complex. Housed inside are football offices, locker rooms, meeting rooms, a strength and conditioning room, a training room, an academic center, a player lounge, and a trophy room.

Following the 1998 season, the track around the football playing field that had hosted the Texas Relays since the 1920s was removed and the track was relocated across the street in the new Mike Myers Track and Soccer Stadium. The field was lowered seven feet, and seats were added. Lowering the field allowed the permanent stadium capacity to grow to 80,638. With the addition of bleachers, stadium capacity soared again, reaching a record crowd of 89,422 during the Ohio State game in 2006.

Significant Stadium Milestones Prior to 1996

- 1924: Texas Memorial Stadium is dedicated.
- 1926: Addition increases north-end capacity to 40,500.
- 1948: Capacity rises to 60,130 with the addition of 26 rows to the east and west sides of the stadium.
- 1955: Lights are added; first night game is played September 17, 1955.
- 1972: West-side upper deck is completed, adding 15,900 seats and bringing capacity to 77,809.

The stadium's east-side upper deck, shown here as completed, was only one of the projects on the drawing board for stadium expansion in the late '90s.

Come Early. Be Loud. Stay Late.

Following the 1998 announcement of Mack Brown's first recruiting class at Texas, he and Sally attended a gathering of Longhorn supporters. The new coach was surprised when more than 3,000 happy fans showed up at what was then Austin Municipal Auditorium.

"We want you to be positive, and we asked you to be patient," Brown told the crowd, which seemed to cheer his every word.

After the event ended, Brown asked his wife, "How did you think it went?"

"Well," Sally Brown replied, "They got that part about being positive—at least for the time being. But that 'patient' part flew right by them."

When he came to Texas, Brown talked to a lot of people about the issues that the Longhorn football program had faced. At the top of the list was complacency among the fans. In response, Brown came up with a slogan designed to empower UT supporters. On a speaking tour of Longhorn Foundation meetings at cities around the state, he encouraged: "Come early. Be loud. Stay late." And then he added, "Wear orange with pride."

Up to that point in UT history, Texas fans had shied away from wearing the burnt orange school color. Many found it to be less than becoming. "I just don't look good in burnt orange," one fan complained to Brown.

"Well," he replied, "Humor me and help us out by wearing it for three or four hours on game day."

As the success of Brown's plan grew, the colors came on. Before Brown came to Texas, it was unusual to see a sea of burnt orange in a stadium. But by the 2005 National Championship game against Southern Cal, the very visible Texas fans outnumbered the Trojan supporters. The College Marketing Service, which represents most colleges and universities, reported that in the 2005 and 2006 seasons, Longhorn merchandise led all schools across the nation in sales.

Brown's advice to come early and be loud took hold with the fans

Texas alumni and fans provide a sea of burnt orange in the stands on game days in Austin.

as well. Texas sold out all of its home games for each of the ten years leading up to and including the 2008 season. And the Longhorn faithful turned Darrell K Royal–Texas Memorial Stadium into one of the loudest facilities in the Big 12 Conference.

Mack Brown and Darrell Royal: Pupil and Mentor

Early in his career, Mack Brown spent several days with a blue ribbon committee as the administrators of Tulane University tried to decide a proper direction for their embattled athletics program. The basketball team had committed egregious NCAA violations, and the football program had awarded only 55 of the 85 scholarships it normally gave. Brown had taken the football job with Tulane in the winter of 1984, assuming athletics director's duties as well. The blue ribbon committee included some of the biggest names in athletics, but the person Brown was most interested in meeting was Darrell Royal.

In their final report on the state of Brown's program, the committee members each offered some positive shred of hope to the young coach. Each of them, that is, except for Darrell Royal. "Son," Royal said, "I would get out of here as fast as you can. You aren't going to get support, and you deserve better. You need to go somewhere where they have 'The' in front of your school's name." His remarks caused the committee's other members to recoil in protest.

"The man hired us to give an opinion, and the least we can do is tell him the truth," Royal replied. Since then, Tulane has made a major commitment to athletics, but at the time, Brown appreciated what Royal said.

It was ironic, then, that a little more than a dozen years later, Mack Brown found himself a candidate for the head football coaching position at the University of Texas. He was eager to reconnect with Royal during the interview process. In fact, he said, "If Coach Royal wasn't going to be there, I wasn't going to meet with them."

The rest, as they say, is history. Royal was a key factor in Brown's decision to come to Texas. But more than that, the two became close friends.

"He told me, 'I don't need another job,'" Brown said of Royal. "'But I will be glad to help where I can.'"

Both men share a commonality in their journey to the head coaching job at Texas. Royal was a star player at Oklahoma and coached at a number of schools, includ-

Brown, seen here during the 2005 national championship season, is a study in concentration, focusing on and intimately involved with the game playing out before him.

Darrell Royal (right) has made himself available to Mack Brown in the new coach's drive to return Texas football to greatness. Nothing says pride like a legend in the locker room.

ing Mississippi State and Washington, before he came to Texas to turn around a program that had gone 1–9 in 1956. Brown was also brought in from the outside to improve a floundering Texas program that had finished 4–7 in 1997.

Royal "takes complicated things and makes them sound simple," Brown said. "He still has a great understanding of the game and has forgotten more football than most of us will ever know."

Brown reached out to Royal and the Longhorn lettermen immediately, founding an annual lettermen's reunion and welcoming Royal and all former players to every practice.

"I asked him when we came, 'What's the best part of coaching football at Texas?'" Brown said.

Royal answered, "Twenty million people care about Texas football."

"So what's the toughest part?" Brown asked.

"Twenty million people care about Texas football."

Brown respectfully referred to their relationship in this way: "He's like an older brother." Once early in Brown's tenure, Royal came by his office and whisked him away to hear a favorite country music star at an afternoon recording session. Brown only agreed to go after Royal assured the new coach that he'd be back in plenty of time for practice.

When Royal spoke to Brown's first senior class just before the 1998 season, he told them that to win, they had to come together "and play as one heartbeat." The phrase became a team motto and the title of two books co-written by Brown.

But perhaps the most accurate advice Royal gave Brown came to its full meaning after the 2005 season and the BCS National Championship win in the 2006 Rose Bowl. When Brown was interviewing for the Texas job, he asked Royal what he believed had been the biggest obstacle to Texas's return to consistent national prominence during the years since he had retired. "The University of Texas," Royal said, "is like a box of BBs. Over the years, the BBs have been dropped, and they have scattered all over the floor. Your job is to get all of the BBs back in the box."

Together, the two coaches have gotten them all back in the box.

When Texas won over the Nebraska Cornhuskers on October 27, 2007, it marked Brown's 100th victory as head coach of the Longhorns. Darrell Royal, who won 167 games at UT, is the only other Longhorn head coach to achieve that milestone.

The Iconic Major Applewhite

To say that Major Applewhite was one of the most popular players in Texas history might be an understatement: Few Longhorns have ever won the hearts of so many fans and the respect of so many opponents.

As a young quarterback, Applewhite attended every football camp he possibly could, which was dedication that paid off when he was recruited by John Mackovic's staff at Texas. He redshirted in 1997 and appeared destined to battle for a backup role in 1998. But an injury to a teammate elevated him into the No. 2 role, and then, as the Longhorns played UCLA at the Rose Bowl in Pasadena in their second game of the season, starting quarterback Richard Walton suffered a year-ending injury to a finger on his throwing hand.

The Longhorns lost that game and then took a 48–7 thrashing by No. 5 Kansas State, but from that point on, Applewhite took charge. With Ricky Williams and capable receivers Kwame Cavill and Wane McGarity in his arsenal, Applewhite led the Longhorns to victory in eight of their next nine games. Only a 42–35 loss at Texas Tech marred an otherwise-perfect record. In tight wins over Baylor, Nebraska, Oklahoma State, and Texas A&M, he proved himself to be a clutch performer during his freshman season. As a sophomore in 1999, he earned honors as the Big 12's co-offensive MVP. But a knee injury in the Cotton Bowl changed Applewhite's career path at Texas.

While recovering, Applewhite alternated with Chris Simms early in the 2000 season, but he again hurt a knee against Texas Tech in a late-season game. He played in a reserve role in 2001, until the second half of the Big 12 championship game against Colorado, when he came off the bench to lead a comeback that fell just short as the 'Horns lost 39–37.

But Applewhite saved his best for last. In the 2001 Culligan Holiday Bowl in San Diego, he struggled early with turnovers but then brought Texas from 19 points behind to a 47–43 victory over Washington. He completed 37 of 55 passes, throwing for 473 yards and four touchdowns to earn offensive MVP honors.

Following his playing career, Applewhite worked two seasons as a graduate assistant at Texas. After serving as an assistant coach at Syracuse and as offensive coordinator at Rice and Alabama, he returned to Texas as the running backs coach for the Longhorns in 2008.

Opposite: *Against Stanford in 1999, sophomore Major Applewhite threw for 353 yards and three touchdowns. The Longhorns prevailed 69–17.* **Below:** *Applewhite waves "Hook 'em, Horns" after taming the Washington Huskies in the 2001 Holiday Bowl in San Diego.*

The 1999 Recruits

Chris Simms and Cory Redding came from different parts of the country, but they arrived with the same goal: to take Texas football to the next level. Simms, the New Jersey–born son of a former star quarterback in the NFL, was named *USA Today*'s high school Offensive Player of the Year in 1998. Cory Redding was from Galena Park North Shore in the Houston area and was named Defensive Player of the Year by the same national newspaper.

Mack Brown's Texas Longhorns finished the 1998 season with a 9–3 record, only a touchdown away from playing for the Big 12 championship. Ricky Williams won the

Defensive end Cory Redding takes on the Colorado Buffaloes. A 39–37 loss to that team in the 2001 Big 12 championship kept the Longhorns from playing for the national championship that year.

Early in his career, Chris Simms often shared the quarter-backing duties, but in 2002 he had the job mostly to himself.

Heisman Trophy—he was in New York City at the same time as Simms was recognized as a high school star by the Downtown Athletic Club of New York.

Simms considered going to a different college, but his visit to Austin charmed him, and he made the decision to attend UT. When Redding also chose Texas, the two players made a pact.

"I remember thinking, 'We are going to do well. With Chris here, we are going to win a lot of games.' I said that, and I believed with everything in my heart that we were going to get a chance to play for a national championship," said Redding.

It was a goal they barely missed in 2001, losing to Colorado by two points in a game where a victory would have earned them a berth in the Rose Bowl, playing for the national championship against Miami.

Simms and Redding were not alone in the class, of course,

Dedicated to Cole Pittman

The recruiting class of '99 had one of the most tragic moments of the Mack Brown era: Teammate Cole Pittman died in February 2001 when his pickup truck crashed into a creek bed as he was returning to Austin from his home in Shreveport.

His locker became a shrine of sorts, and the season's second game was chosen to honor Pittman, No. 44. Before the contest began, his family was presented with a framed No. 44 jersey and other mementos of his time as a Longhorn.

Texas dominated North Carolina in the game that followed, even scoring a safety in the fourth quarter. When Brett Robin ran in a touchdown with 36 seconds on the clock, his six points put the Texas total at 44 points. It didn't take long for the significance of that score to become apparent. Players on the sidelines held up four fingers on each hand to commemorate No. 44. Instead of kicking for an extra point, the Longhorns lined up as if for a two-point conversion. Upon receiving the hiked ball, however, quarterback Major Applewhite kneeled to down it. The game dedicated to Cole Pittman ended with a score of Texas 44, North Carolina 14.

which was voted the No. 1 recruiting class in the nation that spring. Another star was defensive back Nathan Vasher.

The class won 40 games during its tenure at Texas, and Redding, Vasher, and Simms went on to play in the NFL. "We didn't win it all," said Redding, "but we were a part of turning the program around. We came in and made a difference, and that was what mattered."

The number 34 belonged to Ricky Williams his senior year, and 6,279 yards was then the NCAA career rushing record. It remains the career rushing record at UT.

William Mack Brown received this set of spurs from the Silver Spurs Alumni Association when he joined the Longhorns organization. Graced with his initials and the year he first came to Texas, the spurs also feature Texas's longhorn steer symbol.

Santa wearing burnt orange? This young Longhorn cheerleader knows where to go for what she *really* wants for Christmas.

This popular bumper sticker asks a question that doesn't seem to have a satisfactory answer.

If God isn't a Longhorn Why's the sunset Burnt Orange?™

The 2001 Culligan Holiday Bowl trophy belonged to Texas after the 'Horns came back from a 36–17 deficit to the Washington Huskies in the third quarter. The game's final score was 47–43.

The Longhorns beat Oklahoma but not Kansas State in 1999. Their final record for the season was 9–5.

Ricky Williams (No. 11 before his senior year) is immortalized in plastic, diving to get one more yard for his team.

Cracking the BCS in 2004

Wide receiver Tony Jeffery catches a pass from Vince Young for the winning touchdown against Kansas. Texas came from behind to triumph 27–23.

After the Bowl Championship Series began in 1998, Texas was a team on the outskirts of contention. From 1999 through 2003, Texas was the only team in the country consistently ranked in the BCS's final Top 15 standings, but through twists and turns, the Longhorns never quite arrived at the big dance.

In the beginning, only eight teams played in BCS bowls. Six of the spots were reserved for the six conference champions, and the other two were at-large selections. Texas seemed destined to be the hard-luck group among a college football crew of good—bordering on great—teams.

But in 2004, change was in the crisp Texas air. Staff newcomers Greg Robinson and Dick Tomey reworked the Longhorn defense, while offensive co-

ordinator Greg Davis redesigned the offense to feature seasoned running back Cedric Benson, a corps of rookie wide receivers, and quarterback Vince Young.

Young won the starting job during the second half of the 2003 season, and as 2004 began, he showed flashes of the talent that had made him one of the state's top high school recruits in 2002. Benson was the workhorse of the offense, and he teamed with linebacker Derrick Johnson, who was given new responsibilities in Robinson's free-wheeling defense. They were the first Texas players in history to be named national players of the year at their positions in the same season.

The tone of the 2004 season was set in Fayetteville, Arkansas, when the Longhorns came from behind to take the lead. The defense came up with a dramatic turnover to seal a 22–20 victory over the Razorbacks in the second game of the year. Five games later, after a loss to Oklahoma and a shaky performance in a 28–20 win over Missouri, Texas started rolling with a 51–21 victory over Texas Tech in Lubbock. A 31–7 victory over Colorado at Boulder followed. Then came the game that Mack Brown called the defining moment of the era.

Trailing Oklahoma State 35–7 late in the first half, Young led a comeback that electrified the crowd. The defense rose to the moment, and Texas went on to win 56–35. Texas was No. 6 in the national rankings and was battling California and Utah for one of the two at-large bids for the BCS.

This ball commemorates Texas's first-ever appearance in the Rose Bowl in 2005 and its only game to date against Michigan.

As part of the 2005 Rose Bowl festivities, larger-than-life former coaches Darrell Royal of Texas (left) and Bo Schembechler of Michigan appeared together for an interview with ABC Sports.

The confidence the Longhorns gained against Oklahoma State came in handy the following week, when the Longhorns found themselves trailing underdog Kansas late in the game. Texas faced a fourth and 18 near midfield, trailing 23–20 in the closing minute of the game. Vince Young stepped up, out, and into Longhorn immortality. He scrambled for 22 yards and the first down, and then he threw a 21-yard touchdown to Tony Jeffery with 11 seconds to play.

The season was saved, but the BCS berth was in doubt until the final vote of the season, when Texas edged ahead of California and earned the right to play Michigan in the Rose Bowl.

The Longhorns had been to 43 bowl games, but until that time they had never played in the Rose Bowl. The Rose Bowl itself had been an exclusively Big Ten–Pac 10 affair from the late 1940s until it became affiliated with the BCS through its television partner, ABC.

That Rose Bowl game was a conflux of great college football traditions. It marked the first time that Texas and the University of Michigan ever faced off on the football field, and two legendary college football coaches—Darrell Royal of Texas and Bo Schembechler of Michigan—were on hand for the coin flip.

The 93,000-plus fans in the stands blended the burnt orange of Texas and the maize and blue of Michigan. January 1, 2005, was both a celebration of tradition and a showdown of college football.

When Dusty Mangum kicked a 37-yard field goal on the game's final play for a 38–37 Longhorn victory and

quarterback Young found himself on the national stage after his MVP performance, fans called it "the greatest bowl game of its era."

After the game, a reporter pointed out that the national championship game would be in Pasadena the following year. Vince Young proclaimed to the crowd and a national television audience, "We'll be back."

The clock had literally run out by the time Dusty Mangum's kick cleared the goal posts. His successful field goal was all the margin the Longhorns needed to emerge victorious.

The 2005 Dream Season

Several times over Mack Brown's first seven seasons at Texas, his teams were frustratingly close to perfect. When his Longhorns played Nebraska in the 1999 Big 12 championship game, he proclaimed that they were "just visiting" an elite neighborhood of college football champions. His goal, he said, was "to buy a house there."

With the close of the 2004 season in a last-second win over Michigan, Brown's program was validated—his Longhorns were officially part of that elite neighborhood. During 2005, Texas threw an open house and invited the whole world in to celebrate.

Seeking a symbol of the team's commitment to winning all of their games, Brown seized on a passage from the late Harvey Penick, a legendary golf teacher who tutored former Longhorns Ben Crenshaw, Tom Kite, and others. Penick said that to be successful, one must "take dead aim" on a target. Block out everything else. Concentrate on the precision of the vision. Mack Brown created a wristband to remind players of the goal they wanted to achieve, and Texas began its 2005 season by taking dead aim.

With destiny as a traveling companion, the Longhorns started their trek into history during the second game of the season. They faced off against Ohio State in the famed "Horseshoe" in Columbus, marking another first for the Longhorns, who had never played against the Buckeyes. This contest carried all the hype of a bowl game. The

Above: *Wide receiver Limas Sweed takes a fourth-quarter catch into the end zone for a touchdown against Ohio State. The Longhorns won 25–22.*

Longhorns were ranked No. 2, and Ohio State was No. 4. The game lived up to all of the expectations: With just under three minutes remaining, Texas quarterback Vince Young lofted a perfectly thrown pass to a leaping Limas Sweed in the front corner of the end zone for a touchdown. The Longhorns held a 23–22 lead. A late safety and a UT defensive stop clinched the 25–22 Texas victory.

That win kept Texas on pace with No. 1 Southern Cal in a march that lasted the entire regular season. Their next major target was Oklahoma, an opponent that had traditionally been a stumbling block for Longhorn teams. This time, however, Texas crushed the Sooners 45–12. The game was capped by a rumbling 67-yard fumble return for a touchdown by defensive tackle Rod Wright. The 33-point margin equaled the largest ever for Texas in their long rivalry with Oklahoma.

The season also featured another Longhorn come-from-behind win over Oklahoma State, as Vince Young turned in one of the best single-game performances in NCAA history. The Longhorns trailed 28–12 at halftime, but they opened the second half with an 80-yard touchdown run by Young that opened the scoring floodgates. Young became the first player in NCAA history to rush for more than 260 yards and pass for more than 230 yards as he set a UT record of 506 total yards in the 47–28 victory.

The Longhorns averaged more than 50 points per game and finished the regular season by disposing of Baylor, Kansas, and Texas A&M. The highlight of the win over the Aggies was a touchdown pass to fullback Ahmard Hall. Hall—who had served with the Marines in Afghanistan prior to returning to his home state and earning a scholarship at UT after playing as a walk-on—was an inspirational leader for the team.

Texas won the Big 12 Championship by crushing Colorado 70–3 in Reliant Stadium in Houston. Seven Longhorns, including four consensus choices, earned All-America honors. Young won several national awards, including the Maxwell Award, the O'Brien Award, and the Manning Award. Safety Michael Huff became UT's first winner of the Thorpe Award as the nation's best defensive back. Hall, who later signed as a free agent and became the starting fullback for the Tennessee Titans, was given the Distinguished Young American Award by the Greater Austin Chapter of the National Football Foundation and College Hall of Fame.

The Longhorns succeeded in their mission, taking "dead aim" to defeat every opponent, and ended with a 12–0 record. As Big 12 Conference champions, they headed (as promised) back to the Rose Bowl. Their final target was USC—in a game for the national championship.

Quarterback Vince Young searches for an open receiver in this 47–28 win against Oklahoma State.

Reaching Perfection!

The Bowl Championship Series struggled for credibility when it came to anointing its national champion. There were seasons when deserving teams felt they had been left out of the title game and even times when the voters of the Associated Press media poll differed from the team chosen for the BCS game. But in 2005, they definitely got it right.

From the beginning of the season, Southern California and Texas were the No. 1 and No. 2 teams in the nation. The same was true when the BCS standings appeared at midseason. Except for one week, when the two schools switched places, they rode unerringly to a showdown in the BCS national championship game, which was played as the 2006 Rose Bowl in Pasadena's historic stadium. Both teams completed their regular seasons unbeaten. Southern Cal had won 34 straight games, Texas 19.

Most sports classics have a build-up period, but nothing compares to the full month between the end of the regular season and the BCS title game in college football. Early in December, when both Texas and Southern Cal finished their regular seasons unbeaten, the anticipation escalated to enormous proportions. Mack Brown told his team to be careful of their comments, stressing that USC had earned all of the praise the national press was heaping on them.

And then he gave his team a history lesson: The city of Troy had withstood every challenge from the Greeks for ten years, and the city was thought to be impenetrable. Then, the Greeks devised a wooden horse, hid soldiers inside, and graciously appeared to give it to the Trojans. They didn't brag, they didn't talk smack—they simply went in unannounced. Once inside the gates, the Greek soldiers began their fight and took over the place. Brown's plan was to use similar quiet, stealthy cunning to defeat USC.

Meanwhile, USC drew all the media accolades. Cable network ESPN proclaimed the 2005 Trojans the best col-

Safety Michael Griffin intercepts a potential USC touchdown pass in the end zone during the second quarter.

lege football team of all time, and they even ran a series pairing them against the best in the history of the college game.

All the while, Brown and his Longhorns just kept working.

The Heisman Trophy was presented in New York to USC's Reggie Bush. Texas's Vince Young finished second in the voting, and USC's Matt Leinart (the 2004 winner) finished third. Next came the battle of the Rose Bowl tickets. Because the game would be played in the Los Angeles suburb of Pasadena, most people assumed the crowd would heavily favor USC. But somehow when the gates opened, there were more people in the stadium wearing burnt orange than those in USC colors.

As Mack Brown and offensive coordinator Greg Davis stood on the field, Brown looked toward the other end, where they could see Southern Cal warming up.

"That's a really good-looking football team," Brown said.

"Look over here," said Davis, indicating the Longhorns. "There's a pretty good-looking team on our side, too."

Just before kickoff, Mack Brown offered one final piece of advice to his team: "Go out and have fun."

The teams were everything No. 1 and No. 2 should have been. The offenses were relentless, the defenses stubborn. The two most powerful offenses in the country fought for yards, and the defenses surrendered them only grudgingly. Each team resorted to punting only twice in the entire game.

Not even a good tennis match has so many serve-and-return moments. But when the Trojans answered a Texas field goal with a touchdown midway through the fourth quarter, Southern Cal had a 12 point lead at 38–26. Only

six minutes and 42 seconds remained in the Rose Bowl Game for the 2005 national championship.

Young led Texas to a touchdown to cut the lead to 38–33, and then, on the next USC series, the Texas defense, led by Michael Huff, stopped USC near midfield on a fourth-and-two play. Just two minutes and nine seconds remained as Vince Young began a drive that carried the team to the Southern Cal eight-yard line, at fourth down and five.

In the press box, veteran announcer Keith Jackson told America, "Fourth and five at the Trojan 8. This is for the national championship."

After dropping back to pass, Young ran for the corner and scored a touchdown, bringing the score to 39–38 in favor of Texas. A two-point conversion followed. Texas led 41–38, and as the final 19 seconds ticked away, the Longhorns became national champions.

Vince Young dives to slip the ball across the goal line in the third quarter. Young also ran for the dramatic winning touchdown in the game's final minute.

National championship rings come in a variety of styles.

A Longhorn Rose Bowl Red is the perfect wine for any victory celebration.

38-37 Cuvée
Rose Bowl Red

Austin American-Statesman

Thursday, January 5, 2006

statesman.com

THE ROSE BOWL   TEXAS 41, USC 38

50 cents   Final Extra

10 PAGES OF EXPANDED COVERAGE INSIDE

PERFECT FINISH

Young drives Horns to first national championship since 1970

Two words were all that were necessary to convey the triumph of the 2005 season.

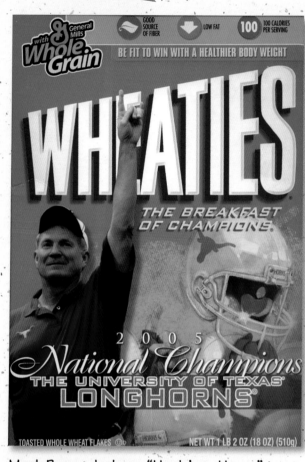

WHEATIES
THE BREAKFAST OF CHAMPIONS.

BE FIT TO WIN WITH A HEALTHIER BODY WEIGHT

GOOD SOURCE OF FIBER   LOW FAT   100 100 CALORIES PER SERVING

2005
National Champions
THE UNIVERSITY OF TEXAS LONGHORNS

TOASTED WHOLE WHEAT FLAKES   NET WT 1 LB 2 OZ (18 OZ) (510g)

Mack Brown declares "Hook 'em, Horns" to the entire nation.

2005 NATIONAL CHAMPIONS
UNIVERSITY OF TEXAS

A championship pennant fits any room decor.

PRESIDENT AND MRS. BUSH
Welcome
THE 2005 NATIONAL CHAMPION
UNIVERSITY OF TEXAS FOOTBALL TEAM

TUESDAY, FEBRUARY 14, 2006
THE WHITE HOUSE

GATES OPEN AT 11:30 A.M.
ARRIVE NO LATER THAN NOON

PHOTO ID REQUIRED   PLEASE ENTER AT SOUTHEAST GATE

A national championship can come with invitations to the White House.

Michael Waltrip drove a real version of this model car at the Texas Motor Speedway in April 2006. Mack Brown was on hand for the race as grand marshal.

The trophies tell the story of Texas's back-to-back Rose Bowl wins.

During spring semester 2006, this T-shirt was the only one a Longhorn student needed.

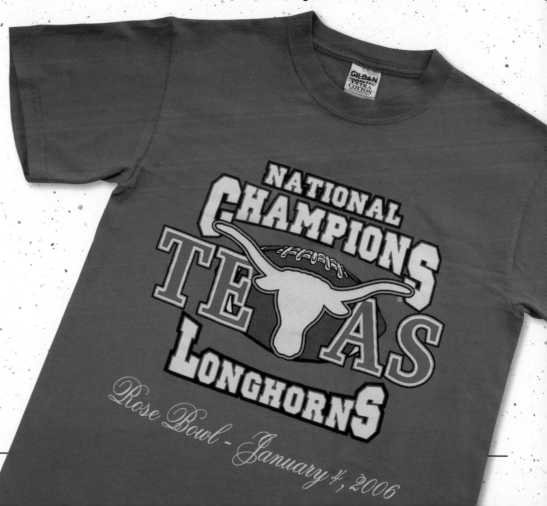

NATIONAL CHAMPIONS
TEXAS
LONGHORNS
Rose Bowl - January 4, 2006

The Amazing Vince Young

Did a triumphant Vince Young deserve his own bobblehead? Yes, he did.

Twenty-one-year-old Vince Young led the Texas Longhorns to a national championship with a spectacular performance in the 2006 Rose Bowl. It was a highlight of his college career. But unlike a Longhorn drive down the field, Young's life path hadn't been smooth.

Vince Young was raised in inner-city Houston. He overcame the adversity of losing friends at a young age, largely thanks to the support of his mother, grandmother, and girlfriend. His faith was strong, and he used it to help develop the talent that led him to his amazing career.

Young was a superstar quarterback at Houston Madison High School but elected to take a redshirt season his first year at Texas in 2002. In 2003, he played as a redshirt freshman, and in 2004 he burst onto the national college football scene.

At 6′6″ and 230 pounds, Young was larger than most players and faster than the others. More significantly, he had natural leadership qualities. He was a pied piper, a proud bearer of his burnt-orange No. 10 jersey.

Coaches saw his talent in practice, but by the middle of his sophomore season of 2004, media and fans began to wonder whether Young's natural talents would be better utilized as a wide receiver. It was then that offensive coordinator Greg Davis and Mack Brown brought him into the film room and showed him footage of some of his high school games, as well as his best

plays at Texas. "This," they said, "is the guy we want. Just go play like that and have fun."

Young took the advice to heart and led his Longhorn team to 20 straight victories. Along the way, he became one of the greatest competitors in the history of the school. Vince Young became a larger-than-life hero. He was a leader, both on and off the field. When his coach needed a sounding board concerning the type of music to be played in the locker room, he turned to Young. When teammates stayed out late or got into some minor trouble, it was Young who would step before the team and tell them to straighten up and remember their goal. He could hug an old man or a kid, and he regularly got a morning phone call from his mother quoting a Bible verse.

Vince Young won every award college football had to offer except the Heisman Trophy, which had gone to USC's Reggie Bush. In its own way, the second-place finish for the Heisman became motivation for Young: He would not lose again. In the Rose Bowl, he passed for nearly 300 yards and ran for another 200, almost replicating his effort on the same Rose Bowl field the year before against Michigan. He had two Rose Bowl MVP trophies and now led the best team in college football.

A few days after the 2006 Rose Bowl, Young declared for the NFL draft, leaving his beloved Texas Longhorns with their first national title in 35 years. A year later, playing for the Tennessee Titans, he became the first rookie quarterback in league history to go to the Pro Bowl.

Vince Young came to the University of Texas as an extremely talented athlete who played quarterback. He left Texas an extremely talented quarterback who was an athlete.

Opposite: Young looks for some open field as he breaks away from USC defenders.

Supporting High School Coaches

Mack Brown's earliest memory of a high school coach was riding a school bus with his grandfather, who was the winningest school coach in Middle Tennessee history. Brown's feet couldn't reach the floor, but he was decked out in his own special letter jacket.

So when he was hired as the Texas Longhorn football coach, it wasn't hard for Brown to respond to a suggestion from Darrell Royal. "Call Eddie Joseph," Royal said. "He's the executive director of the Texas High School Coaches Association. You need to ask him if it's okay for you to coach in this state."

Brown shares Royal's respect for high school coaches. Since coming to Texas, he has formed a special bond with those who teach young kids.

The Texas High School Coaches Association is the largest body of its kind. Its annual summer clinic draws as many as 13,000 coaches, representatives of the more than 1,500 high schools in the state. Eddie Joseph, who has since retired, was a former high school coach himself, and because of Brown's strong commitment to members of the coaches' organization, he became a big Texas fan.

The Longhorn football staff annually hosts a spring clinic, attended by almost 1,000 coaches. The program includes top collegiate coaches from around the country, as well as the coaches whose teams won state championships in the various divisions of the University Interscholastic League playoffs.

When the Longhorns won the 2005 national championship over Southern Cal, Brown publicly thanked the high school coaches for their work in preparing young players for college. As his recruiting base has expanded, Brown has broadened his comments to include high school coaches from across the country. But his heart, and his loyalty, will always be strongly tied to Texas.

When the TV series *Friday Night Lights* (which features high school football in a small Texas town) was being taped in Austin, Brown and Joseph agreed to appear in the series pilot. It was another example of how much high school football means in Texas and how much it means to Mack Brown.

Mack Brown talks with Hugh Sandifer of Abilene at a Texas Longhorns clinic for high school football coaches, which the university hosts annually each spring.

Turning on the Star Power

One of the interesting sidelights of the Longhorns' meeting with Southern California in the 2005 BCS national championship game in the Rose Bowl was a showdown of "star power."

The Trojans have long been known as an attraction for movie stars from the Los Angeles area, and BCS officials were actually concerned about a sideline crowded with high-profile USC supporters. So they enacted a rule that each team could have only four sideline passes for celebrities. Neither team wanted to pick their top four stars, and as far as Texas was concerned, that was just fine.

Country singer and Longhorns fan LeAnn Rimes performs the national anthem before the 2006 Rose Bowl.

How, UT officials wondered, could they choose between golfing greats Ben Crenshaw and Tom Kite? It was a given that seven-time Cy Young–winner Roger Clemens would be there, as well as popular actor Matthew McConaughey. When Mack and Sally Brown first moved to Austin, cycling star Lance Armstrong was their neighbor, so Texas could count on him, too. And what about soccer star Mia Hamm, who had been a friend of the Browns since the days when she was a college student at North Carolina?

Actor Rex Linn, who is part of the cast of TV's *CSI: Miami,* may be the Longhorns' biggest fan in Hollywood (next to McConaughey), and national anthem singer LeAnn Rimes snuck Mack Brown a "Hook 'em, Horns" sign as she hurried off the field to change into burnt orange. The Longhorns could have produced a good contingent of NFL players, or stars from the TV series *Friday Night Lights.* Singer George Strait, a friend of Darrell Royal, has been a frequent visitor to Longhorn home games.

The most prominent Longhorn fan, however, wasn't at the Rose Bowl at all—he was back home in the White House in Washington, D.C. President George W. Bush had worked out in the Longhorns' strength-and-conditioning room while he was governor of Texas, and he maintained a close friendship with Brown. At 6 A.M., just as Brown was nodding off to sleep in the early morning hours following the Rose Bowl victory, his telephone rang. It was 9 A.M. in Washington, and the president had been up for hours, just waiting to call and congratulate him.

A month later, the entire Longhorn team and traveling party visited the White House, where President Bush honored the 2005 national champions of college football.

Lance Armstrong (left) and Matthew McConaughey celebrate with the Longhorns after their BCS national championship win.

Colt McCoy Takes Up the Mantle

If ever anybody was born to be a Texas football quarterback, it was Colt McCoy. His dad, Brad, made sure of that while his mother Deborah was in the delivery room in a New Mexico hospital. Brad slipped a tray of Texas soil under her bed.

In the 1940s, there was Bobby Layne. James Street was the hero of the Wishbone in the last part of the 1960s, following a guy named Duke Carlisle, who quarterbacked the national champions of 1963. But in an age of high-tech passing games and running quarterbacks, McCoy came from a tiny West Texas town to become the starting quarterback in the post–Vince Young era at Texas. In his first three years with the Longhorns, he earned his spurs as one of the greatest of the Longhorn signal callers.

Starting as a redshirt freshman in 2006, McCoy tied an NCAA record for touchdown passes by a freshman and earned honors as *The Sporting News*'s National Freshman of the Year. By the time he led the Longhorns to a 12–1 season and a 24–21 victory over Ohio State in the Tostitos Fiesta Bowl in his junior year, he had become the winningest quarterback in Texas history, posting a 32–7 record with his senior season yet to come.

He set a single-season NCAA completion percentage record of 76.7 percent in 2008, capping the year off with a record-setting 41 completions of 59 attempts for 414 yards as he earned the Fiesta Bowl's Most Valuable Offensive Player Award. In his already-loaded trophy case, McCoy keeps offensive MVP awards from the Longhorn wins in the 2006 Alamo Bowl and the 2007 Pacific Life Holiday Bowl.

McCoy was the Associated Press 2008 Big 12 Offensive Player of the Year and a first team All-American. Active in community service, he is a member of the American Football Coaches Association Good Works team.

In 2008, McCoy was named national Player of the Year by the Walter Camp Foundation and finished as runner-up for both the Heisman Trophy and the Maxwell Award.

The Future at DKR

It all began as a dream, a plan to create a monument to war heroes and a sufficient stadium in which to play the game of college football in Texas. And as Darrell K Royal–Texas Memorial Stadium turned 84 years old, its look changed dramatically.

With the crash of a steel ball following the 2006 season, the stadium's north end, which had stood for 80 years after its construction in 1926, came tumbling down. In its place rose a north end-zone facility that added seats and stadium suites and completely changed the dynamic of the stadium.

Rising from the rubble of the old bricks and broken concrete of the original facility, a new lower stand and an upper deck were constructed. The new facility links the east and west sides of the stadium, matching the look of the completed east stands. A new visitor's locker room, television compounds, and gymnasiums were included in the project, which also features a museum and food court open to the public year-round.

The revised seating arrangement raised the base seating capacity of the stadium to more than 90,000, and with the addition of portable bleachers in the south end, the Longhorns were able to achieve a record crowd of 98,621 for their 2008 season-finale game against Texas A&M. Following the season, work began on an addition to the Moncrief-Neuhaus Complex at the south end that will include a state-of-the-art football academic center, as well as new bleacher seats that will take stadium capacity to more than 100,000—making it not only the largest stadium in the southwestern part of the United States but, by the start of the 2009 season, the fifth largest in the country.

The "Memorial" in Darrell K Royal–Texas Memorial Stadium has also become fully realized, with a special area recognizing the veterans who fought in the armed forces of the United States in all foreign conflicts from World War I through the more recent conflict in Iraq.

As it is, the latest upgrades to the stadium give the University of Texas a state-of-the-art facility that represents the campus, the football program, and all those who bleed orange as they move forward in the 21st century.

Construction was completed and Darrell K Royal–Texas Memorial Stadium was open and ready for business in 2008. Rooters in attendance certainly saw an exciting season they'll long remember.

The Unexpected Season of 2008

Senior Chris Ogbonnaya, in only his second career start, carried the ball 15 times for 127 yards against Oklahoma. His 62-yard run in the fourth quarter helped set up the final Longhorn touchdown in this 45–35 victory.

The 2008 football season at the University of Texas began with a theme: "You have to be consistently good to be great." And the players' success and consistency produced one of the greatest teams in Longhorn history.

Capping the year with a No. 3 national ranking, a 12–1 season, and a victory over Ohio State in the Tostitos Fiesta Bowl, the team—picked to finish in the middle of the pack of the six-team South Division of the Big 12—came within one second of earning a chance to play for the national championship. The 12 victories were the second-most ever for a UT team, trailing only the 2005 national champions, and the bowl win over Ohio State marked the Longhorns' third BCS game win in a five-year period and the seventh bowl triumph in an eight-year span.

While observers in the Big 12 considered this a rebuilding year for Texas, the 'Horns began the season ranked No. 10 nationally but quickly went on a steady rise. When UT defeated nationally top-ranked Oklahoma in Dallas 45–35, Texas moved to the No. 1 spot—for the first time during the regular season since 1984. That was also their first game in a quest for a feat that hadn't been accomplished since the 1940s—conquering four straight teams ranked in the Top 10. And they almost made it. Following the win over Oklahoma, Texas slammed Missouri, which had been ranked No. 2 only a week before, 56–31. Next came No. 7 Oklahoma State, which Texas beat 28–24. The only glitch in the season occurred the week after that in Lubbock. After the Longhorns had staged a dramatic rally to take a 33–32 lead with 1:29 left, No. 6 Texas Tech scored again with only one second left on the clock to end the UT streak.

Texas shrugged off the loss by crushing Baylor, Kansas, and Texas A&M by a combined score of 129–37. But when the Big 12 South ended in a three-way tie among Texas, Texas Tech, and Oklahoma, the league's tiebreaker went to the team that finished highest in the

BCS standings. Going into the final week, that had been Texas, but Oklahoma wound up edging the 'Horns by .0128 point—and the Sooners were granted the right to play in the Big 12 championship game.

Disappointed but still determined, Texas took its No. 3 national ranking to Phoenix to meet No. 10–ranked Ohio State in the Tostitos Fiesta Bowl, and in the Valley of the Sun, the stars came out for the Longhorns. Throwing for a personal-best 414 yards and leading the Longhorns on a winning drive in the final two minutes, quarterback Colt McCoy led his team to a 24–21 victory over the Buckeyes. The game winner came with 16 seconds remaining on a 26-yard scoring pass from McCoy to receiver Quan Cosby, who caught 14 passes in the game. The defense, led by MVP Roy Miller and national award-winner Brian Orakpo, stopped Ohio State one last time to preserve the victory.

McCoy, who set an NCAA Division I record for pass completion percentage, was named the Fiesta Bowl MVP as he won a UT-best 32nd game as a starting quarterback.

The unexpected season was as heartwarming as it was gratifying, as the Longhorns of 2008 became not only one of the best but one of the most popular teams in school history. The Fiesta Bowl win was the 201st victory in Mack Brown's 25-year career as a head coach at Appalachian State, Tulane, North Carolina, and Texas. His 11th season at Texas also marked a year in which the Longhorns passed Notre Dame as the second-winningest team in NCAA history.

Not only did the 2008 Longhorns post victories over five teams that, at some point during the season, were ranked in the nation's Top 20, the team also excelled in the classroom. Of the team's 23 seniors, all but 3 had achieved their undergraduate degrees by the time the 'Horns played Ohio State, and those 3 were on track to graduate in the spring.

The final No. 3 ranking in the *USA Today*/Coaches Poll placed the Longhorns among the top Texas teams of all time. McCoy and his receivers Cosby and Jordan Shipley set all kinds of offensive records, and Orakpo won the Nagurski Trophy and the Lombardi and Hendricks awards all within five days of earning his degree in December.

With consistency and character, the 2008 team reached their goal. In the end, despite a couple of tough breaks that would have sidetracked others, they kept their composure and their determination, and they will be remembered as one of the greatest Longhorn teams ever.

Texas and Ohio State traded the lead more than once in the Fiesta Bowl. Wide receiver Quan Cosby, seen here ahead of OSU's Marcus Freeman, scored a Longhorn touchdown with 16 seconds on the clock, making the final score 24–21.

Small children who sleep with a Longhorn plush toy know they will be protected all through the night.

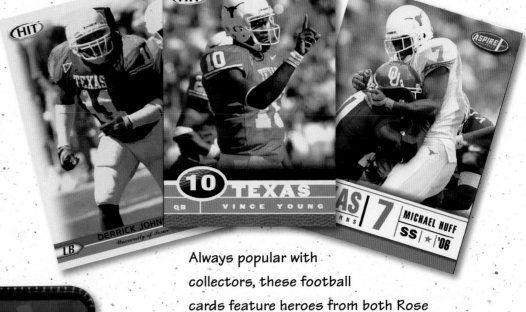

Always popular with collectors, these football cards feature heroes from both Rose Bowl victories.

Even Mr. Potato Head wants to join the team. Note that the ten pieces included are indentified as "hard hitting."

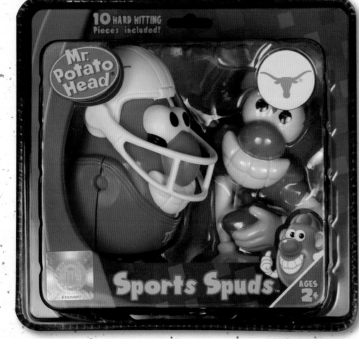

Simple. Elegant. Classic. A Texas Longhorns patch adds just the right touch to a oollege hoodie.

Is Texas due for another national championship? This Longhorn bobblehead is certain to nod its head yes.

Get alumni parties rocking with a drumstick and this piece of Texas Longhorn percussion. More cowbell!

BASEBALL COLUMN

By Anup Shah
Daily Texan
Columnist

Baseball Coach Augie Garrido should 'pay' for his DWI arrest

It's bound to happen. On a college campus known around the world for its partying and drinking, student athletes are going to find themselves in trouble with the law. It's inevitable.

But early Saturday morning, Texas baseball coach Augie Garrido was arrested and charged with suspicion of driving under the influence. Athletic director DeLoss Dodds suspended Garrido indefinitely with pay.

As a baseball coach, Garrido is brilliant. If there's any coach at Texas who can keep his team looking directly ahead at the next game, or who can keep his team's head up in a winless slump, it's Augie. The guy knows people. He knows how to get his players to trust him.

But that's also why Garrido's suspension is so much worse than it appears on the surface. Garrido is a role model. People can learn so much from him by just listening to him talk. He's one of the most rational people anyone can be around. He gets it.

It's one thing for a Texas athlete to get a DUI. They're young. Like all of us, they make mistakes and learn from them. But Garrido will be 70 in less than a month. With 1,668 wins, he has more Division I victories than any other coach in NCAA baseball history.

And worst of all, the incident comes at a time when the Longhorns are starting a new season, trying to pull themselves out of a slump. Since the 2005 College World Series win, the Longhorns have yet to re-

TEXAS 24   Tostitos FIESTA BOWL   OHIO STATE 21

Above, Senior Roy Miller embraces Colt McCoy following the Longhorns' comeback victory over Ohio State in the Fiesta Bowl on Jan. 5. **Below,** Senior Quan Cosby leaps across the goal line after he catches a McCoy pass across the middle. Cosby's touchdown put Texas up 24-21 with less than a minute left.

Jeffrey McWhorter | Daily Texan Staff

Seniors lift Texas in thrilling bowl win

By Brad Gray
Daily Texan Staff

GLENDALE, Ariz. — With less than a minute remaining in the Tostitos Fiesta Bowl, Texas quarterback

ONLINE: Poto gallery from the game at dailytexanonline.com

And when the Buckeyes attempted to

Texas opened its 2007 season against Arkansas State at home. The 21–13 win marked its ninth victory in ten season openers.

The Daily Texan, UT's student newspaper, focused on the human side of the Longhorns' 2009 Fiesta Bowl win, spotlighting defensive MVP Roy Miller's celebration with offensive MVP Colt McCoy.

Texas Through the Years

Annual Records, 1893–2008

Year	Overall Record				Conference Record				Year	Overall Record				Conference Record			
	W	L	T	%	W	L	T	%		W	L	T	%	W	L	T	%
1893	4	0	0	1.000	—	—	—	—	1921	6	1	1	.813	1	0	1	.750
1894	6	1	0	.857	—	—	—	—	1922	7	2	0	.778	2	1	0	.667
1895	5	0	0	1.000	—	—	—	—	1923	8	0	1	.944	2	0	1	.833
1896	4	2	1	.643	—	—	—	—	1924	5	3	1	.611	2	3	0	.400
1897	6	2	0	.750	—	—	—	—	1925	6	2	1	.722	2	1	1	.625
1898	5	1	0	.833	—	—	—	—	1926	5	4	0	.556	2	2	0	.500
1899	6	2	0	.750	—	—	—	—	1927	6	2	1	.722	2	2	1	.500
1900	6	0	0	1.000	—	—	—	—	1928	7	2	0	.778	5	1	0	.833
1901	8	2	1	.773	—	—	—	—	1929	5	2	2	.667	2	2	2	.500
1902	6	3	1	.650	—	—	—	—	1930	8	1	1	.850	4	1	0	.800
1903	5	1	2	.750	—	—	—	—	1931	6	4	0	.600	2	3	0	.400
1904	6	2	0	.750	—	—	—	—	1932	8	2	0	.800	5	1	0	.833
1905	5	4	0	.556	—	—	—	—	1933	4	5	2	.500	2	3	1	.417
1906	9	1	0	.900	—	—	—	—	1934	7	2	1	.750	4	1	1	.750
1907	6	1	1	.813	—	—	—	—	1935	4	6	0	.400	1	5	0	.167
1908	5	4	0	.556	—	—	—	—	1936	2	6	1	.278	1	5	0	.167
1909	4	3	1	.563	—	—	—	—	1937	2	6	1	.278	1	5	0	.167
1910	6	2	0	.750	—	—	—	—	1938	1	8	0	.111	1	5	0	.167
1911	5	2	0	.714	—	—	—	—	1939	5	4	0	.556	3	3	0	.500
1912	7	1	0	.875	—	—	—	—	1940	8	2	0	.800	4	2	0	.667
1913	7	1	0	.875	—	—	—	—	1941	8	1	1	.850	4	1	1	.750
1914	8	0	0	1.000	—	—	—	—	1942	9	2	0	.818	5	1	0	.833
1915	6	3	0	.667	2	2	0	.500	1943	7	1	1	.833	5	0	0	1.000
1916	7	2	0	.778	5	1	0	.833	1944	5	4	0	.556	3	2	0	.600
1917	4	4	0	.500	2	3	0	.400	1945	10	1	0	.909	5	1	0	.833
1918	9	0	0	1.000	4	0	0	1.000	1946	8	2	0	.800	4	2	0	.667
1919	6	3	0	.667	3	2	0	.600	1947	10	1	0	.909	5	1	0	.833
1920	9	0	0	1.000	5	0	0	1.000	1948	7	3	1	.682	4	1	1	.750

Year	Overall Record				Conference Record				Year	Overall Record				Conference Record			
	W	L	T	%	W	L	T	%		W	L	T	%	W	L	T	%
1949	6	4	0	.600	3	3	0	.600	1987	7	5	0	.583	5	2	0	.571
1950	9	2	0	.818	6	0	0	1.000	1988	4	7	0	.364	2	5	0	.286
1951	7	3	0	.700	3	3	0	.500	1989	5	6	0	.455	4	4	0	.500
1952	9	2	0	.818	6	0	0	1.000	1990	10	2	0	.833	8	0	0	1.000
1953	7	3	0	.700	5	1	0	.833	1991	5	6	0	.455	4	4	0	.500
1954	4	5	1	.450	2	3	1	.417	1992	6	5	0	.545	4	3	0	.571
1955	5	5	0	.500	4	2	0	.667	1993	5	5	1	.500	5	2	0	.714
1956	1	9	0	.100	0	6	0	.000	1994	8	4	0	.667	4	3	0	.571
1957	6	4	1	.591	4	1	1	.750	1995	10	2	1	.808	7	0	0	1.000
1958	7	3	0	.700	3	3	0	.500	1996	8	5	0	.615	6	2	0	.750
1959	9	2	0	.818	5	1	0	.833	1997	4	7	0	.364	2	6	0	.250
1960	7	3	1	.682	5	2	0	.714	1998	9	3	0	.750	6	2	0	.750
1961	10	1	0	.909	6	1	0	.857	1999	9	5	0	.643	6	2	0	.750
1962	9	1	1	.864	6	0	1	.929	2000	9	3	0	.750	7	1	0	.875
1963	11	0	0	1.000	7	0	0	1.000	2001	11	2	0	.846	7	1	0	.875
1964	10	1	0	.909	6	1	0	.857	2002	11	2	0	.846	6	2	0	.750
1965	6	4	0	.600	3	4	0	.429	2003	10	3	0	.769	7	1	0	.875
1966	7	4	0	.636	5	2	0	.714	2004	12	1	0	.923	7	1	0	.875
1967	6	4	0	.600	4	3	0	.571	2005	13	0	0	1.000	8	0	0	1.000
1968	9	1	1	.864	6	1	0	.857	2006	10	3	0	.769	6	2	0	.750
1969	11	0	0	1.000	7	0	0	1.000	2007	10	3	0	.769	5	3	0	.625
1970	10	1	0	.909	7	0	0	1.000	2008	12	1	0	.923	7	1	0	.875
1971	8	3	0	.727	6	1	0	.857									
1972	10	1	0	.909	7	0	0	1.000									
1973	8	3	0	.727	7	0	0	1.000									
1974	8	4	0	.667	5	2	0	.571									
1975	10	2	0	.833	6	1	0	.857									
1976	5	5	1	.500	4	4	0	.500									
1977	11	1	0	.927	8	0	0	1.000									
1978	9	3	0	.750	6	2	0	.750									
1979	9	3	0	.750	6	2	0	.750									
1980	7	5	0	.583	4	4	0	.500									
1981	10	1	1	.875	6	1	1	.813									
1982	9	3	0	.750	7	1	0	.875									
1983	11	1	0	.927	8	0	0	1.000									
1984	7	4	1	.625	5	3	0	.625									
1985	8	4	0	.667	6	2	0	.750									
1986	5	6	0	.455	4	4	0	.500									

Coaches

No coach	1893	4–0–0	1.000
R. D. Wentworth	1894	6–1–0	.857
Frank Crawford	1895	5–0–0	1.000
Harry Robinson	1896	4–2–1	.643
F. W. Kelly	1897	6–2–0	.750
D. F. Edwards	1898	5–1–0	.833
M. G. Clarke	1899	6–2–0	.750
S. H. Thompson	1900–1901	14–2–1	.853
J. B. Hart	1902	6–3–1	.650
Ralph Hutchinson	1903–5	16–7–2	.680
H. R. Schenker	1906	9–1–0	.900
W. E. Metzenthin	1907–8	11–5–1	.677
Dexter Draper	1909	4–3–1	.563
W. S. Wasmund	1910	6–2–0	.750

Dave Allerdice	1911–15	33–7–0	.825
Eugene Van Gent	1916	7–2–0	.778
Bill Juneau	1917–19	19–7–0	.731
Berry Whitaker	1920–22	22–3–1	.865
E. J. Stewart	1923–26	24–9–3	.708
Clyde Littlefield	1927–33	44–18–6	.691
Jack Chevigny	1934–36	13–14–2	.483
Dana X. Bible	1937–46	63–31–3	.665
Blair Cherry	1947–50	32–10–1	.756
Ed Price	1951–56	33–27–1	.549
Darrell Royal	1957–76	167–47–5	.774
Fred Akers	1977–86	86–31–2	.731
David McWilliams	1987–91	31–26–0	.544
John Mackovic	1992–97	41–28–2	.592
Mack Brown	1998–	115–26–0	.816

Bowl Games

Season	Bowl Game	Result
1942	Cotton Bowl	Texas 14, Georgia Tech 7
1943	Cotton Bowl	Texas 7, Randolph Field 7
1945	Cotton Bowl	Texas 40, Missouri 27
1947	Sugar Bowl	Texas 27, Alabama 7
1948	Orange Bowl	Texas 41, Georgia 28
1950	Cotton Bowl	Tennessee 20, Texas 14
1952	Cotton Bowl	Texas 16, Tennessee 0
1957	Sugar Bowl	Mississippi 39, Texas 7
1959	Cotton Bowl	Syracuse 23, Texas 14
1960	Bluebonnet Bowl	Texas 3, Alabama 3
1961	Cotton Bowl	Texas 12, Mississippi 7
1962	Cotton Bowl	LSU 13, Texas 0
1963	Cotton Bowl	Texas 28, Navy 6
1964	Orange Bowl	Texas 21, Alabama 17
1966	Bluebonnet Bowl	Texas 19, Mississippi 0
1968	Cotton Bowl	Texas 36, Tennessee 13
1969	Cotton Bowl	Texas 21, Notre Dame 17
1970	Cotton Bowl	Notre Dame 24, Texas 11
1971	Cotton Bowl	Penn State 30, Texas 6
1972	Cotton Bowl	Texas 17, Alabama 13
1973	Cotton Bowl	Nebraska 19, Texas 3
1974	Gator Bowl	Auburn 27, Texas 3

Season	Bowl Game	Result
1975	Bluebonnet Bowl	Texas 38, Colorado 21
1977	Cotton Bowl	Notre Dame 38, Texas 10
1978	Sun Bowl	Texas 42, Maryland 0
1979	Sun Bowl	Washington 14, Texas 7
1980	Bluebonnet Bowl	North Carolina 16, Texas 7
1981	Cotton Bowl	Texas 14, Alabama 12
1982	Sun Bowl	North Carolina 26, Texas 10
1983	Cotton Bowl	Georgia 10, Texas 9
1984	Freedom Bowl	Iowa 55, Texas 17
1985	Bluebonnet Bowl	Air Force 24, Texas 16
1987	Bluebonnet Bowl	Texas 32, Pittsburgh 27
1990	Cotton Bowl	Miami 46, Texas 3
1994	Sun Bowl	Texas 35, North Carolina 31
1995	Sugar Bowl	Virginia Tech 28, Texas 10
1996	Fiesta Bowl	Penn State 38, Texas 15
1998	Cotton Bowl	Texas 38, Mississippi State 11
1999	Cotton Bowl	Arkansas 27, Texas 6
2000	Holiday Bowl	Oregon 35, Texas 30
2001	Holiday Bowl	Texas 47, Washington 43
2002	Cotton Bowl	Texas 35, LSU 20
2003	Holiday Bowl	Washington State 28, Texas 20
2004	Rose Bowl	Texas 38, Michigan 37
2005	Rose Bowl	Texas 41, USC 38
2006	Alamo Bowl	Texas 26, Iowa 24
2007	Holiday Bowl	Texas 52, Arizona State 34
2008	Fiesta Bowl	Texas 24, Ohio State 21

Heisman Trophy Winners

Earl Campbell 1972   Ricky Williams 1998

Top 10 in Heisman Trophy Balloting

Jack Crain, 10th in 1941
Bobby Layne, 8th in 1946; 6th in 1947
James Saxton, 3rd in 1961
Scott Appleton, 5th in 1963
Tommy Nobis, 7th in 1965
Chris Gilbert, 8th in 1968
Steve Worster, 4th in 1970
Roosevelt Leaks, 3rd in 1973
Kenneth Sims, 8th in 1981
Ricky Williams, 5th in 1997
Cedric Benson, 6th in 2004
Vince Young, 2nd in 2005
Colt McCoy, 2nd in 2008

National Championships

| 1963 | (AP, UPI) | 1970 | (UPI) |
| 1969 | (AP, UPI) | 2005 | (AP) |

Consensus First-Team All-Americans

Scott Appleton, T - 1963
Bill Atessis, DE - 1970
Hub Bechtol, DE - 1945, '46
Justin Blalock, OT - 2006
Tony Brackens, DE - 1995
Earl Campbell, RB - 1977
Leonard Davis, OT - 2000
Doug Dawson, OG - 1983
Tony Degrate, DT - 1984
Derrick Dockery, OG/T - 2002
Chris Gilbert, RB - 1968
Jerry Gray, DB - 1983, '84
Glen Halsell, LB - 1969
Casey Hampton, DT - 2000
Michael Huff, S - 2005
Quentin Jammer, CB - 2001
Derrick Johnson, LB - 2003, '04
Johnnie Johnson, DB - 1978, '79
Bobby Layne, QB - 1947
Roosevelt Leaks, RB - 1973
Jeff Leiding, LB - 1983

Carlton Massey, DE - 1953
Colt McCoy, QB - 2008
Bud McFadin, G - 1950
Bob McKay, OT - 1969
Steve McMichael, DT - 1979
Dan Neil, OG - 1996
Tommy Nobis, G/LB - 1965
Brian Orakpo, DL - 2008
James Saxton, RB - 1961
Jonathan Scott, OT - 2005
Bob Simmons, OT - 1975
Kenneth Sims, DT - 1980, '81
Jerry Sisemore, OT - 1971, '72
Terry Tausch, OT - 1981
Johnny Treadwell, G - 1962
Ricky Williams, RB - 1997, '98
Steve Worster, FB - 1970
Rod Wright, DT - 2005
Bob Wuensch, OT - 1970
Bill Wyman, C - 1973
Vince Young, QB - 2005

Longhorns in the College Football Hall of Fame

Hub Bechtol
Dana X. Bible
Earl Campbell
Chris Gilbert
Johnnie Johnson
Malcolm Kutner

Bobby Layne
Roosevelt Leaks
Bud McFadin
Tommy Nobis
Darrell Royal
James Saxton

Harley Sewell
Jerry Sisemore
Mortimer "Bud" Sprague
Harrison Stafford

Award Winners

Butkus Award
Derrick Johnson, 2004

Doak Walker Award
| Ricky Williams, 1997 | Ricky Williams, 1998 | Cedric Benson, 2004 |

Draddy Trophy
Dallas Griffin, 2007

Lombardi Award
| Kenneth Sims, 1981 | Tony Degrate, 1984 | Brian Orakpo, 2008 |

Maxwell Award
| Tommy Nobis, 1965 | Ricky Williams, 1998 | Vince Young, 2005 |

Davey O'Brien National Quarterback Award
Vince Young, 2005

Davey O'Brien Memorial Trophy
Earl Campbell, 1977

Outland Trophy
| Scott Appleton, 1963 | Tommy Nobis, 1965 | Brad Shearer, 1977 |

Jim Thorpe Award
| Michael Huff, 2005 | Aaron Ross, 2006 |

Walter Camp Player of the Year Award
Colt McCoy, 2008

Texas Rushing Records

Most Rushing Yards
Game	350	Ricky Williams, vs. Iowa State	1998
Season	2,124	Ricky Williams	1998
Career	6,279	Ricky Williams	1995–98

Most Rushing Touchdowns
Game	6	Ricky Williams, vs. New Mexico State/Rice	1998
Season	27	Ricky Williams	1998
Career	72	Ricky Williams	1995–98

Texas Passing Records

Most Passing Yards

Game	473	Major Applewhite, vs. Washington	2001
Season	3,859	Colt McCoy	2008
Career	9,732	Colt McCoy	2006–

Most Passing Completions

Game	41	Colt McCoy, vs. Ohio State (*Fiesta Bowl*)	2009
Season	332	Colt McCoy	2008
Career	825	Colt McCoy	2006–

Most Touchdown Passes

Game	6	Colt McCoy, vs. Baylor	2006
Season	34	Colt McCoy	2008
Career	85	Colt McCoy	2006–

Longest Pass Play

97 yards	Major Applewhite to Wane McGarity, vs. Oklahoma	1998

Texas Receiving Records

Most Pass Receptions

Game	13	Roy Williams, at Nebraska	2002
Season	100	Kwame Cavil	1999
Career	241	Roy Williams	2000–2003

Most Touchdown Receptions

Game	4	Wane McGarity, vs. Texas Tech	1998
Season	12	Limas Sweed	2006
		Roy Williams	2002
Career	36	Roy Williams	2000–2003

Most Interceptions

Game	4	Bill Bradley, vs. Texas A&M	1968
Season	7	Nathan Vasher	2001
	7	Jerry Gray	1984
	7	William Graham	1981
	7	Jack Crain	1940
	7	Noble Doss	1940
Career	17	Nathan Vasher	2000–2003
	17	Noble Doss	1939–41

Longest Interception Return for Touchdown

95 yards	Jack Collins, vs. Baylor	1936

Most Receiving Yards

Game	198	Johnny "Lam" Jones, vs. Baylor	1979
Season	1,188	Kwame Cavil	1999
Career	3,866	Roy Williams	2000–2003

Texas Defense Records

Most Total Tackles
(tackles were recorded as a statistic beginning in 1975)

Season	195	Britt Hager	1988
Career	499	Britt Hager	1984–88

Most Sacks
(sacks were recorded as a statistic beginning in 1975)

Season	22.5	Kiki DeAyala	1982
Career	40.5	Kiki DeAyala	1979–82

Other Texas Records

Points Scored

Game	36	Ricky Williams, vs. New Mexico St./Rice	1998
Season	168	Ricky Williams	1998
Career	452	Ricky Williams	1995–98

Most Kickoff Return Yards

Game	159	Quan Cosby, vs. Texas A&M	2007
Season	1,017	Quan Cosby	2007
Career	1,731	Quan Cosby	2005–8

Most Punt Return Yards

Game	173	Nathan Vasher, vs. Baylor	2001
Season	554	Nathan Vasher	2001
Career	1,314	Nathan Vasher	2000–2003

Most Field Goals Made

Game	5	Ryan Bailey at UCF	2007
	5	Kris Stockton at Texas Tech	2000
	5	Jeff Ward at Arkansas	1985
Season	22	Kris Stockton	2000
Career	59	Phil Dawson	1994–97

Index

A

Akers, Fred: accepts Texas job, 82; Darrell Royal and, 99; Earl Campbell and, 84–85; 1977 season, 83, 88; 1983 season, 91; recruiting, 89; under fire, 92, 93, 96, 103

Akins, Marty, 76, 77

Alderson, C. J. "Shorty," 17

Aldridge, Thomas, 93

Allerdice, Dave, 12

Allred, James V., 21

Andrews, Billy "Rooster," 36–37, 51

Ansley, Sam, 83

Appleton, Scott, 52–53, 54

Applewhite, Major, 114–15, 117

Armstrong, Lance, 131

Atessis, Bill, 72

Aune, Jon, 83

B

Bechtol, Hub, 36

Bell, Matty, 30

Bellard, Emory, 58

Bellmont, L. Theo, 14, 16

Benson, Cedric, 120

Bertelsen, Jim, 66, 72

Bevo, 15, 30, 43

Bible, Dana X.: accepts Texas job, 24–25; as athletics director, 46; Bobby Layne and, 36–37; during World War II, 32; formality of, 22; Immortal 13 and, 29; influence of, 6, 38, 40, 92; 1937 season, 33; 1938 season, 26; 1941 season, 30–31; recruiting, 28

Blanton, Ox, 17

Brabham, Danny, 50

Bradley, Bill, 57, 58, 65

Broeg, Bob, 52

Brown, James, 101

Brown, Mack: accepts Texas job, 106–7; auto racing and, 127; Cole Pittman and, 117; Darrell Royal and, 112–13; famous fans and, 131; Foreword, 6–7; Freddie Steinmark Scoreboard and, 68; "Hook 'em, Horns" and, 41; 1998 season, 116; on Wheaties box, 126; relationship with Texas high

Brown, Mack (continued) school coaches,130; Ricky Williams and, 108–9; school colors and, 51, 111; spurs of, 118; 2004 season, 120; 2005 national championship, 104, 124–25; 2005 season, 122; 2009 Fiesta Bowl, 135; Vince Young and, 128

Brown, Sally, 6, 106–7, 108, 111, 131

Broyles, Frank, 27, 67, 73, 77

Bryant, Bob, 48

Bryant, Paul "Bear," 6, 56, 76, 78

Bush, George H. W., 67

Bush, George W., 131

Bush, Reggie, 125, 128

Butts, Wally, 6

Byrd, D. Harold, 41

C

Cade, Mossy, 91

Camp, Walter, 10

Campbell, Ann, 85

Campbell, Earl, 62, 77, 80, 82, 83, 84–85, 87, 109

Campbell, Mike, 47, 63, 65, 82, 96

Carlisle, Duke, 52, 132

Cavill, Kwame, 114

Cherry, Blair, 34, 37, 38–39, 40

Chevigny, Jack, 20–21, 22, 24, 28, 40

Clark, Harley, 41

Clark, Roy, 67

College Football Hall of Fame, 17, 36, 57, 59, 77, 83, 85, 123

Collins, Spot, 46

Comer, Deryl, 59

Connally, John, 52–53

Cook, Beano, 66–67

Cosby, Quan, 135

Crain, Jack, 28, 29, 30

Crawford, Walt, 10

Crow, John David, 24, 47, 109

Culpepper, Pat, 50

Currie, Tom, 56

Curry, E. A., 62

D

Dabbs, Ken, 85

Dale, Billy, 72

Daniel, Chal, 29

Daugherty, Duffy, 46

Davis, Gilly, 26

Davis, Greg, 120, 125, 128

Dawson, Doug, 91

Day, Addison, 10

Degrate, Tony, 91

Dicus, Chuck, 68

Di Nino, Vincent R., 54

Disch, William J. "Billy," 12, 20

Dixon, Joe, 50

Dodd, Bobby, 6, 46

Dodds, DeLoss, 92, 96, 107

Dolley, J. C., 24–25

Dorsett, Tony, 109

Doss, Noble, 28, 29, 30–31

Duncum, Duane, 93

Dyer, Ben, 15

E

Edmond, James "Pete," 16

Elkins, Wilson "Bull," 17

Ellington, Bill, 63, 92

Emerson, Ox, 17

Erwin, Frank C., Jr., 53, 64, 74

Evans, Wilbur, 30, 69

F

Field, Jackie, 34

Ford, Tommy, 50, 53

Frank, D. A., 11

Freeman, Denne H., 79

Freeman, Marcus, 135

Furman, Dave, 10

G

Garrett, Julian, 29

Gautt, Prentice, 76

Gilbert, Chris, 57, 58–59

Graham, Billy, 67

Gray, Jack, 19

Gray, Jerry, 91

Griffin, Michael, 124

Griffith, J. M. "Miz Griff," 30

Grob, Reggie, 50

Guest, Edgar, 29

Gustafson, Cliff, 65

H

Hall, Ahmard, 123

Halsell, Glenn, 72

Hardin, Wayne, 53

Hatchett, Derrick, 89

Hayes, Robert "Bullet Bob," 88

Heard, Robert, 61, 94

Henderson, Scott, 72

Herskowitz, Mickey, 58

Higginbotham, James, 16

Hilliard, Bohn, 19, 21

Hipple, Augusta, 31

Holmes, Priest, 100, 101

Hudson, Jim, 56

Huff, Michael, 123, 125

J

Jackson, Alfred, 83
Jackson, Bo, 93
Jackson, Keith, 125
Jeffery, Tony, 120, 121
Johnson, Derrick, 120
Johnson, Johnnie, 77, 83, 89
Johnson, Lyndon Baines, 53, 62
Jones, Howard, 25
Jones, James Carroll "T," 47, 92
Jones, Johnny "Ham," 88
Jones, Johnny "Lam," 83, 88, 89
Jones, Tony, 97
Jordan, Louis, 16
Joseph, Eddie, 130

K

Kane, Bothwell, 16
Kaye, Linda, 69
Kelsey, Mike, 50
Kennedy, John F., 52
Kimbrough, John, 29
Koy, Ernie, 6, 17, 56
Koy, Ernie, Jr., 6
Koy, Ted, 6, 58, 67, 69, 72
Kristynik, Marvin, 56
Kutner, Malcolm, 28, 31

L

Lackey, Bobby, 48
Landry, Tom, 99
Layden, Pete, 23, 28, 29, 30–31
Layne, Bobby, 36–37, 38, 132
Leahy, Frank, 42, 46
Leaks, Roosevelt, 62, 77, 84
Lee, Dick, 10
Lee, Robert E., 11

Leiding, Jeff, 91
Leinart, Matt, 125
Lemons, Abe, 92
Lewis, Derek, 80–81, 101
Little, Donnie, 89
Littlefield, Clyde, 12–13, 17, 20, 51
Longhorn Hall of Honor, 11, 37, 63, 83
Lowry, Alan, 77

M

MacArthur, Douglas, 53
Mackovic, John, 99, 100–101, 106, 114
Mangum, Dusty, 121
Marshall, Keifer, 32
Martin, Vernon, 29
Mather, W. T., 14
Mauldin, Stan, 32
McBath, Mark, 83
McConaughey, Matthew, 131
McCoy, Colt, 132, 135, 137
McEachern, Randy, 83
McFadin, Louis "Bud," 35
McGarity, Wane, 114
McKay, Roy Dale, 32, 34
McLane, Paul, 10
McLane, Ray, 10
McLean, Bill, 10
McMichael, Steve, 89
McWilliams, David, 53, 96–97, 99, 102, 103
Metcalf, Eric, 97
Miller, Roy, 135, 137
Mitchell, Bobby, 68
Montana, Joe, 83
Moore, Victor, 10
Morenz, Shea, 101
Morrison, Jim, 10
Morrison, Ray, 25
Myers, "Baby," 10

N

Nabors, Rick, 68
Namath, Joe, 56, 60
National Football League Hall of Fame, 37, 85
Nixon, Richard M., 67, 70, 78
Nobis, Tommy, 56, 57
Norton, Homer, 29
Norwood, Joe, 58

O

Ogbonnaya, Chris, 134
O'Neal, Leon, 62
Orakpo, Brian, 135
Osborne, Tom, 91

P

Parseghian, Ara, 69
Parsons, Robinson, 62
Patrick, R. B., 28
Patterson, Gary, 103
Penick, Harvey, 122
Peterson, Lester, 17
Philip, John, 10
Phillips, Eddie, 58, 72–73, 76
Pinckney, Stephen, 15
Pittman, Cole, 117
Pittman, Jim, 47
Pitts, Henry, 41
Prather, William Lambdin, 11
Price, Edwin Booth, 40
Prothro, Tommy, 72

R

Redding, Cory, 116–17
Reeves, Henry, 11
Renfro, Mel, 50
Richardson, Billy, 10
Rimes, LeAnn, 131
Robin, Brett, 117
Robinson, Greg, 120

Robnett, Marshall, 29
Rochs, Bob, 32
Rockne, Knute, 12, 20
Rogers, Lorene, 82
Roosevelt, Theodore, 12
Roy, Robert, 10
Royal, Darrell: accepts Texas job, 46–47; assistant coaches and, 63; Earl Campbell and, 84–85; early years at Texas, 48–49; end of coaching career, 76–77; Freddie Steinmark and, 68; influence of, 6–7, 80, 82, 96, 99, 104; James Street and, 65; Johnny "Lam" Jones and, 88; kneeling on sidelines, 44–45; Mack Brown and, 106–7, 112–13, 130; memorabilia, 55, 60; mid-1960s doldrums, 57; national championships, 71; 1963 national championship, 52–53; 1965 Orange Bowl, 56; 1970 Cotton Bowl, 69; 1970 season, 72–73; on record album, 78; recruiting, 62; relationship with boosters, 51; rivalry with Arkansas, 27, 50, 67; Royalisms of, 61, 75; stadium construction and, 74; stadium named for, 110; 2005 Rose Bowl and, 121; winning percentage of, 93;

Royal, Darrell (continued) wishbone offense and, 58
Royal, Edith, 46

S

Samuels, Chris, 98
Sanders, Spec, 30
Sandifer, Hugh, 130
Sauer, George, 56
Saxton, James, 49
Schembechler, Bo, 67, 121
Schenkel, Chris, 66
Schulze, Bob, 47
Scovell, Field, 69
Shearer, Brad, 83
Shelley, Dexter, 17
Sherrill, Jackie, 93
Shipley, Jordan, 135
Shira, Charley, 47
Shivers, Allan, 82
Simmons, Edwin, 90–91
Simmons, Paul, 13
Simms, Chris, 114, 116–17
Sinclair, John, 11
Sisemore, Jerry, 77
Sloan, Steve, 56
Smartt, Joe, 21
Speyrer, Charles "Cotton," 59, 61, 69, 72–73
Stafford, Bret, 97
Stafford, Harrison, 17
Stagg, Amos Alonzo, 19, 25
Stark, H. J. Lutcher, 11
Staubach, Roger, 53
Steinbeck, John, 46
Steinmark, Freddie, 68
Street, Huston, 65
Street, James, 58–59, 61, 65, 67, 69, 72, 132
Swarthout, Jack, 47
Sweatt, Hemann, 62

Sweed, Limas, 122–23
Switzer, Barry, 107

T

Talbert, Charles, 52
Texas High School Coaches Association, 130
Theismann, Joe, 69
Thomas, David, 105
Thompson, Neils, 74
Tomey, Dick, 120
Treadwell, Johnny, 50

V

Vasher, Nathan, 117
Vaught, Johnny, 17

W

Wacker, Jim, 82
Walker, Adrian, 98
Walker, Doak, 37, 38, 109
Walton, Richard, 114
Waltrip, Michael, 127
Ward, Jeff, 91
Warmath, Murray, 46
Warner, Pop, 25
Wasmund, Billy, 12
Whittier, Julius, 62
Wigginton, Donnie, 76
Wilkinson, Bud, 47, 48, 66
Williams, Ricky, 108–9, 114, 116, 118, 119
Willsey, Ray, 47
Woodard, Tommy, 73
Worster, Steve, 57, 58–59, 61, 71, 72–73
Wright, Rod, 123
Wuensch, Bobby, 72

Y

Young, Vince, 105, 120–21, 123, 125, 128–29, 132